GW00493898

First published in 2010
© Demos. Some rights reserved
Magdalen House, 136 Tooley Street
London, SE1 2TU, UK

ISBN 978–1–906693–35–0
Copy edited by Susannah Wight
Series design by Modernactivity, London
Typeset by Modernactivity
Printed by Lecturis, Eindhoven

Set in Gotham Rounded
and Baskerville 10
Cover paper: Arctic Volume
Text paper: Munken Print White

ALL TOGETHER:
A CREATIVE APPROACH TO
ORGANISATIONAL CHANGE

Robert Hewison
John Holden
Samuel Jones

DEMOS

The person who has nothing to learn is certainly incapable of creative dialogue.

Michael Boyd, 20 June 2008

Leaders are only as good as the people they lead

Vikki Heywood, January 2010

Contents

Acknowledgements

We would like to thank the entire staff of the Royal
Shakespeare Company, and the many people who have helped
with our research over the last three years. In particular, we
wish to thank Sir Christopher Bland, Michael Boyd, Adele
Cope, Vikki Heywood, Andrew Parker and Liz Thompson.
For their help throughout, we would also like to thank Lyndon
Jones, Michele Percy, Kirstin Peltonen and Carol Stevenson.
Libby Alexander and Mary Butlin were also helpful in
sourcing material relating to human resources and ticket sales.

We have also worked closely and had many discussions
with the expert on organisational development, Dr Mee-Yan
Cheung-Judge, and have drawn on her wisdom and knowledge
about organisations and leadership. In steering group
meetings, we have benefited from the comments of Hilary
Carty, Jon Kingsbury and Angela Pugh.

A number of interns at Demos provided valuable
assistance with this project. They are Nic Mackay, Kacie
Desmond, Amarjit Lahel, Elaine Cronin, Kiley Arroyo and
Tobias Chapple.

Robert Hewison
John Holden
Samuel Jones

March 2010

Sponsors' forewords

The Cultural Leadership Programme

The Cultural Leadership Programme works to strengthen leadership practice in the cultural sector and our range of programmes and opportunities are complemented by advocacy, discourse and original research. These underpin the shifts in individual practice and organisational change that arise through sustained investment in leadership development. The sector is diverse and eclectic – one size does not fit all, so the navigation of different models and approaches to leadership is essential.

What seems clear is that the next paradigm in leadership demands both a philosophical and a systems-based shift in leadership practice. In contemporary organisations, leadership is being tested, negotiated and earned in a dynamic interchange of authority between 'leaders' and 'followers'. So the opportunity to support the Royal Shakespeare Company on its journey through 'ensemble' leadership stood out as a key priority for the Cultural Leadership Programme.

This publication describes a journey that has stimulated and challenged the organisation. Routemaps have to be revised as the realities of people, the organisation and change impact on plans and expectations. As such, this research offers a valuable viewing gallery into the dynamic reality of leading creative organisations in the twenty-first century – vital insights that will undoubtedly resonate for other organisations and sectors.

Hilary Carty
Director, Cultural Leadership Programme

NESTA

The UK's world-beating creative sector is living through one of its most exciting periods. At the heart of this renaissance is a return to what we value so much about the sector – its relentless desire to reinvent itself, tread new ground and push the boundaries of what can be achieved. This is what has always made us distinct.

Performing arts organisations have been a critical part of this renaissance. And like other creative businesses – in film, video games, music or architecture – they are not exempt from the opportunities or challenges posed by digitisation and globalisation. That is why it's so critical that we invest in trials and conduct experiments that open up new, more effective and creative ways of working. They will not only lead to the growth and sustainability of the performing arts, they will also allow other parts of the sector and, indeed, the wider economy to benefit from their lessons.

The Royal Shakespeare Company (RSC) has lived up to its innovative and dynamic reputation by adopting an 'ensemble' approach. Reflecting what we already know about innovation – that at its heart lies a process of bringing together powerful combinations of people, resources and bright ideas to spearhead change – the RSC has developed expertise in how innovation can create a thriving, twenty-first century cultural organisation.

The information captured in this report is important because it helps ensure that what we've learnt about business innovation in cultural organisations can be shared with others. Getting the right balance of innovative practices, the need for strong leadership, and a realisation that creative success is not hindered but enhanced by collaboration across a whole organisation are all themes that emerge from this work.

NESTA, for its part, has been delighted to offer its insights and guidance to this programme, and we will work hard to ensure that its lessons can be widely scaled and adopted.

Jonathan Kestenbaum
CEO of NESTA

Executive summary

This report was commissioned by the Royal Shakespeare
Company (RSC) in February 2007. The RSC had embarked
on a major programme of change in the way it is led and
managed, to mirror the physical transformation of its home in
Stratford-upon-Avon. The RSC wished to extend the principles
of ensemble, as applied to the acting company, to the whole
organisation, in both its internal management and external
relations. This would be carried out by the management of the
RSC, advised by the consultant Dr Mee-Yan Cheung-Judge.
The cultural team at the think tank Demos was asked to
follow this journey, observing the process and reporting back
through this publication. The RSC hopes that the experiences
recorded might be useful to other cultural organisations as
well as the wider business community.

The concept of ensemble
Historically the RSC has described itself as an ensemble – a
French word meaning 'together' or 'viewed as a whole'. In
the theatre, it has the specific meaning of a group of actors
who work together in a collaborative fashion over a period
of time. Over the last three years the leadership of the RSC
has sought to extend what they describe as the 'usefully
ambiguous' idea of ensemble beyond the rehearsal room
and the acting company into the whole organisation. The
principle has been used to bring about changes in attitudes,
behaviours and practices.

    Ensemble should be thought of not only as a
management tool, but as a set of moral principles that remains
constant as a guide to leadership decisions and administrative
actions. Ensemble is a value, as well as a description of a

particular way of organising people: a way of being as much as a way of doing. It is also a moving target in that it can be rearticulated to meet changing needs and circumstances.

The principle of ensemble as an organisational practice

Organisations need to build systems that are not just optimally efficient in a specific set of circumstances, but capable of changing to meet new circumstances: in other words, organisations need internally generated resilience. In turn, that resilience is generated by creating shared terms of engagement – they cannot be imposed – that govern the relationships between different people and functions.

It is the job of leaders to develop both organisational interconnectedness, and the capacity of individuals and departments to work together. Instead of attempting the now impossible task of micromanaging specialised, knowledge-driven functions, leaders must pay attention to developing the norms of responsibility, honesty and trust within the organisation that enable people to work together.

Ensemble addresses exactly these questions of instilling behavioural norms through strong values, while reconciling the individual's needs for creative expression, reward, and liberty, with the need to be part of a social system that is efficient, responsive and liberating rather than conformist, restricting and inefficient.

Results of the application of the ensemble principle at the RSC

Organisational development, guided by ensemble principles has helped the RSC to achieve artistic success, improved financial performance and morale, and made operations and productions more efficient.

Leadership has played an essential role in aligning the values of ensemble with strategic objectives and organisational change. This has been achieved by employing rhetorical power and judicious intervention, and by balancing organic evolution with an intentional programme of change.

Change is a continuous process, not an event. Most organisational change succeeds after five years, if at all (it is estimated that 75 per cent of attempts to change organisations fail).[1] At the RSC, significant progress has been observed after two and a half years, although the company still feels that there is more to learn and do, and wants to extend the principle of ensemble to its relationship with audiences.

Internal change processes need to align with external conditions. Creating a common understanding of external expectations of the organisation is one essential function of leadership.

Some of the organisational changes that have happened at the RSC are conventional, though not necessarily easy to achieve: improved communications; delegated responsibilities; more transparency; greater resilience; accessible leaders. Other aspects of the RSC's development are less conventional and offer useful lessons.

Distinctive lessons learned
Emotions are important – acknowledge them
A remarkable feature of the RSC's leadership and management style has been the regular and explicit reference to emotions. Very few leaders in government or the corporate sector speak openly about the emotions that everyone knows are a major feature of organisational life.

Leaders are at the heart of a network, not at the top of a pyramid
As Henry Mintzberg puts it, 'a robust community requires a form of leadership quite different from the models that have it driving transformation from the top. Community leaders see themselves as being in the centre, reaching out rather than down.'[2]

The realisation of creativity rests on collaboration
As a leading cultural organisation, the RSC lives and breathes artistic creativity. But every organisation has to adapt, innovate and be creative to some degree. The RSC's experience shows that creativity can only be realised through collective and collaborative endeavour, and the more that is facilitated – through good communications, a strong common culture, the creation of the right set of attitudes and so on – the more likely it is that an organisation will be able to experiment, and hence to innovate well, across its whole range of activities.

Conceptual simplicity is the best response to organisational and contextual complexity
Every large-scale organisation is complex, and every organisation exists within a changing and multifaceted context. Difficult and demanding tasks need to be underpinned by clear and comprehensible concepts that everyone understands and can feel part of, both intellectually and emotionally. The RSC is a compelling example of a complex organisation with a simple message: when asked what was the purpose of the RSC, our interviewees repeatedly expressed the same aspiration: to be the best theatre company for Shakespeare in the world.

Prologue: the conditions for creativity

5 January 2009

Michael Boyd, Artistic Director of the Royal Shakespeare Company, is at the entrance to the RSC's rehearsal studios in Clapham, South London, greeting actors as they arrive at the start of their first day's work on a contract that will run through to 2011 with the option to extend to 2012. Vikki Heywood, the RSC's Executive Director, is also there, preparing to introduce the actors to the organisation in which they will work.

Actors, along with production and administrative staff and observers, arrange themselves on chairs in a wide circle and, in turn, say who they are. After formal welcomes, Boyd and Heywood speak of the challenges ahead.

The RSC's physical home in Stratford-upon-Avon, the Royal Shakespeare Theatre (RST), is being reconstructed. But so is the organisation that will occupy it, because a complete revision of the RSC's management systems has been under way for the last three years. Guided by the principle on which the RSC was founded, and which Boyd and Heywood are committed to rediscovering, the proposition is that the whole RSC should be an ensemble.

Once Boyd has laid out the plans for the coming three years, it is the main topic of his welcoming speech:

We have found that this approach to theatre-making both enables and requires a set of behaviours worth looking at, because they create our conditions – what we call the conditions for creativity. And they also create the conditions for community.

The report that follows explores what 'ensemble' could mean to organisations within and beyond the cultural sector. It looks at the relevance of ensemble to the task of, in the words of the renowned business academic Henry Mintzberg, 'building companies as communities'.[3]

About this report

In February 2007 Demos was engaged to observe and report on the process through which the RSC had begun to change the way that it is organised and led. The RSC's organisational development is directed towards fulfilling its artistic purpose, improving the experience that it offers its current and future audiences, and making it a better place in which to work.

This report is part history, part commentary, and partly the articulation of lessons. What it is not is an evaluation. In 2007, the RSC had no baseline or end-point for its organisational development. On the contrary, it saw organisational development as a never-ending, dynamic process: something that must happen on a continuous basis because people come and go, projects move on, and operating contexts shift.

Much of our understanding about the RSC has come from an extensive range of interviews and conversations, with present and former staff members of the RSC at all levels and in most operating areas: actors, former leaders of the organisation, the Chair of the RSC board, other board members and Shakespeare scholars. In particular, we conducted 57 in-depth interviews with 45 staff at an interval of 24 months in order to judge progress. A complete list of interviewees is included in appendix 1. We were able to observe some of the externally facilitated workshops held at the RSC that were part of the organisational development process, and were present at internal meetings and a board away day. We were also able to observe rehearsals. Our presence within the organisation provided opportunities for self-reflection for those involved in the process, as people had to articulate their thoughts to us in interviews.

We have read widely about the theatre and the practice of ensemble, and have consulted the RSC's extensive archive of newspaper commentary and reviews of their productions. In addition, we have examined various historical documents relating to the RSC including books, articles, the RSC's Strategic Plan, annual reports, management accounts, and board minutes from 2000 to 2008. We have also applied organisational and leadership theory to what we have seen, and studied a number of other companies such as The Eden Project, Google, Pixar and South West Airlines.

As observers, we have tried not to interfere with what was happening at the RSC, but the very fact that we were invited to witness the change process is, in itself, significant, because it shows that the RSC was willing to be transparent and courageous. Not all organisations welcome outside scrutiny of their vulnerable moments.

A note on terminology

In this report the word 'company' refers to a group of actors and associated production staff working on a production. The word 'organisation' refers to employees of the Royal Shakespeare Company as a whole.

The word 'director' refers to the director of a theatrical production, unless a different function, such as 'Finance and Administration' is attached.

The word 'ensemble' is used both as an adjective and as a noun.

1 Changes and challenges at the RSC

The value of the RSC's story is as an example of a company in turnaround.
Sir Christopher Bland, Chairman of the Board of Governors of the RSC, February 2009.

This chapter gives a brief description of the RSC and the crisis that prompted a change of leadership and strategic direction in 2002/03. It also outlines the changing social and technological context in which organisations have to operate. Internal and external changes have led to the process of organisational development described in this report.

The Royal Shakespeare Company

The Royal Shakespeare Company is the best-known theatre company in the world, and has a long and distinguished history. It traces its origins to the building of the Shakespeare Memorial Theatre in Stratford-upon-Avon in 1879. It became the Royal Shakespeare Company in 1961 under the direction of Peter Hall who in 1960 had established it as an 'ensemble' company, performing both in Stratford-upon-Avon and at the Aldwych Theatre in London. It rapidly became a flagship cultural organisation for the UK of major national and international importance, performing new plays as well as the classical repertoire. In 1977, having played in a number of additional, smaller venues in London, it established what is now the Donmar Warehouse as a second London stage, where the focus was on new plays and the modern repertoire. In 1982 it moved all its London work into the newly opened Barbican Theatre, where it remained until 2002. Under the successive artistic leadership of Hall, Trevor Nunn, Terry Hands, Adrian

Noble and now Michael Boyd, it has presented the works of Shakespeare as a living part of our cultural heritage, and been the training ground for at least three generations of theatre professionals including actors, directors and designers, many of whom have become household names.

The RSC is a charitable, not-for-profit organisation, with a Royal Charter. His Royal Highness the Prince of Wales is President of a governing body of, at the time of writing, 37 Governors, but day-to-day oversight is exercised by the 16 members of the board, led by the Chairman, currently Sir Christopher Bland. Two members of the RSC's executive staff are on the board: Michael Boyd, the Artistic Director, and Vikki Heywood, the Executive Director. All board members are also Governors of the RSC.

As the name implies, the RSC exists to play Shakespeare, but always in a contemporary context. Shakespeare is presented alongside a classic canon, and the RSC has consistently performed modern plays and commissioned new work.

The RSC is based at the Royal Shakespeare Theatre (RST) in Stratford-upon-Avon, a medium sized town in Warwickshire approximately 100 miles from London. At the time of writing in 2009, the RSC is reaching the end of a substantial remodelling of both the main stage and auditorium of the RST, and the public spaces that envelop them. Both before and after the current building programme the RSC would normally run three theatres in Stratford: the RST, The Swan and a third, smaller space, The Other Place.

The purpose of the RSC is to produce great work for the widest possible audience. Everything that it does is directed to this end. It brings to this task considerable strengths: royal patronage, an experienced and committed board, a proud history, an excellent reputation and dedicated staff, many with years of experience in the craft and skills of the theatre. The RSC has a valuable and respected brand name and enjoys considerable public support and affection. A recent brand audit commissioned by the RSC showed that it is the most recognised theatre name in the UK.

1999—2002: a period of crisis

The RSC began the twenty-first century facing serious
challenges to its operating model, compounded by misguided
leadership, internal dissension and low morale. Many of the
conditions that led to this situation had been developing for
years, and were exposed when, between 1999 and 2002, the
RSC experienced a crisis that threatened to overwhelm it, and
manifested itself in a number of areas.

Governance

The governance structure had become outmoded and
inefficient. Before 1999 there had been no board between the
management and a large group of Governors. A board was
put in place in 1999 but the relationship between it and the
organisation had yet to mature.

Management

The RSC was managed on strictly hierarchical lines. Artistic
decisions were taken by a small group of senior creatives
around the Artistic Director, and operational decisions
focused at this time on the Managing Director. The Finance
Director closely controlled all budgets, and under the
direction of the Managing Director, the Human Resources
Department managed the staff centrally. Emblematically, the
row of offices occupied by senior management was known
as 'the corridor of power'. An Arts Council appraisal carried
out in 1990 had warned that the management of the RSC
was unusually centralised, and that communications within
the organisation were poor.[4] At a board meeting in 2003, the
newly appointed Artistic Director Michael Boyd summed up
the problem:

*The RSC has suffered both historically and in the recent past from
a remote and overly hierarchical management approach which has
led to a sclerosis in the communication of authority, the misuse of
information as power and a dearth of initiative and management
skills at departmental level.[5]*

The erosion of the acting ensemble

By 2000 the ensemble principle, as applied to the acting company, had been undermined by changes in the theatrical economy that meant that many actors were reluctant to take long-term contracts. It is also possible that the RSC's poor critical reputation at this time and the working conditions in the company, discouraged long-term commitment. At the same time, the leadership of the RSC respected the principle of ensemble acting less, since it was argued that it constrained the choice of talent to work with.

External relationships

Relations with the RSC's principal public funder, Arts Council England (ACE), were severely strained. In 1999, the RSC entered the Arts Council's Stabilisation Programme. This was intended to create a financial breathing space for arts organisations in difficulties while they reorganised their policies, management structures and finances. Normally, stabilisation programmes were developed in concert with ACE, but the senior management of the RSC developed their plans independently, advised pro bono, and in extreme secrecy, by a team of management consultants from McKinsey. Their plan became known as Project Fleet.

Failed reform

Project Fleet did not cause the crisis that threatened to engulf the RSC, but its effect was to make the crisis worse. Two decisions taken at the time, to leave the Barbican, the RSC's London home since 1982, and to rebuild the RST, have in fact been carried through, although the approach to transforming the RST has been different, and the timetable altered. The Project Fleet plan was over-optimistic on several fronts: about the possibility of RSC productions being presented in London on an ad hoc basis in different venues by commercial managements; about help from the USA in fundraising and production partnerships with American universities; and about the ability to raise an endowment. Significantly, Project Fleet proposed to weaken the ensemble principle in the acting company, with actors' contracts limited to six to nine months, at most. Overall, the plan had been to introduce a spirit of enterprise by exploiting the RSC brand. At that time, however, the brand was a waning asset.

Morale
Project Fleet called for 85 redundancies in London and up to 60 in Stratford-upon-Avon. The redundancies resulting from the departure from the Barbican affected staff morale – especially since the RSC had long been thought of as a 'family' by many people working there – and damaged trade union relationships. These redundancies were carried out at the decision of the Managing Director through a centralised human resources process, and were announced at a large company meeting that circumstances had obliged the management to hold.

Finance
Although the RSC has substantial capital resources in the form of land and buildings, like all performing arts organisations, it is dependent on a combination of box-office and other earned revenue including commercial transfers, donations, commercial sponsorship, and public subsidy, chiefly from ACE. Critical reputation also has a profound influence on financial success. In 2000, financial projections showed that the RSC would soon be facing an annual deficit of £4 million.

During the period 1999–2002, the simultaneous pressures of delivering Project Fleet and the projected rebuilding of the RST proved too much for the overstretched staff. While the need for change was recognised, the staff of the RSC could not support a plan that had been sprung on them. Loyal senior staff were left to drive through a top-level decision. The theatrical profession denounced the plans as a destruction of everything the RSC was supposed to stand for, as was widely reported in the press at the time.[6] There was a public protest march in Stratford-upon-Avon, and strikes were only narrowly averted.

While the RSC and ACE tried to find a way forward, in 2002 the then Artistic Director exercised his contractual right to take a sabbatical in order to direct a West End musical, *Chitty Chitty Bang Bang*. In April 2002, he announced that he would not be seeking renewal of his contract, which expired in April 2003.

It should be noted that the RSC was not the only cultural organisation facing significant financial and operational problems at the close of the 1990s. The Royal Opera House, the British Museum, English National Opera and others were also in severe difficulties. Post 2000, the operating context for the arts improved: funding increased, a number of iconic buildings were opened, and, before the recession of 2008/09, there was a fresh spirit of confidence.

The changing context for institutions

In parallel with the immediate problems of the RSC, social and technological developments were (and still are) combining to change the way that organisations, including the RSC, must operate:

- Technology has made communication quicker, and increased the connectivity (the number, strength, speed and frequency of connections) between people within organisations and between institutions.
- The speed at which organisations need to function, in order to remain competitive in the face of changing consumer expectations and rapidly changing externalities, means there is no longer time for decisions to flow up and down hierarchies making the devolution of decision making essential.
- There is an increasing tendency to put together teams and ad hoc groupings of people from both within an organisation and outside it to solve specific problems, or to address specific issues that require particular combinations of knowledge, skill or access to networks for their solution.
- In order to reduce costs and use expertise efficiently, organisations are outsourcing more of the functions that used to be managed and developed in-house.

- As roles within organisations have become increasingly specialised, and ever more complex within those specialisms, it has become impossible for leaders to know everything about their organisations. They can no longer be the ultimate source of knowledge.
- A further consequence of increased specialisation is that particular skills and competencies become highly valued, and 'talent retention' can become difficult. People are motivated to stay with organisations not only by financial reward, but by finding satisfaction and emotional reward in their work and their working relationships.
- Organisations now operate in virtual as well as physical spaces. Consumers can interact with organisations, and staff members can be managed, out of hours and without face-to-face contact. This not only places new demands on staff in terms of their knowledge, skills and behaviour, but also means that more people within organisations are now 'frontline' because they have direct contact with the outside world. In turn, this presents challenges in terms of communications, brand management, logistics and investment.

These developments combine to create a situation in which organisations need to build systems that are not just optimally efficient in a specific set of circumstances, but also capable of changing to meet new circumstances: in other words, organisations need internally generated resilience. In turn, that resilience is developed by creating shared terms of engagement – they cannot be imposed – that govern the relationships between different people and functions.

It is the job of leaders to develop organisational interconnectedness, and the capability of individuals and departments to work together. Instead of attempting the now impossible task of micromanaging specialised, knowledge-driven functions, leaders must pay attention to developing the norms of responsibility, honesty and trust within the organisation that enable people to work together.

The RSC believes that the ensemble principle addresses exactly these questions of instilling behavioural norms through strong values while reconciling the individual's needs for creative expression, reward, and autonomy, with the need to be part of a social system that is efficient, responsive and liberating rather than conformist, restricting and inefficient.

The challenges faced by the RSC

The events of 1999–2002 precipitated the change process at the RSC that began with the appointment of Michael Boyd as Artistic Director in 2002 (with effect from April 2003), and which is still continuing. Now, as in 2002, the RSC's management has to find solutions to two sets of challenges, one generic to any organisation in transition, and the other specific to the RSC. The principal challenges facing the RSC are scale and complexity and organisational ageing.

Scale and complexity

As of 31 December 2009, a total of 807 people were employed in varying capacities by the RSC. They included:

- 384 permanent employees
- 87 people on long-term contracts
- 126 actors and stage managers
- 131 pro-rata musicians (whose employment varies from regular to very occasional work)
- 79 casual workers.

The RSC normally performs year-round across three stages in Stratford-upon-Avon, has an annual residency in Newcastle, mounts seasons in London, and presents national and international tours. During the period covered by this report reconstruction work at Stratford meant that performances there were confined to one temporary theatre, The Courtyard. This means that the number of productions, performances and potential audience numbers in Stratford were constrained and, in normal circumstances, would be considerably larger.

In 2008/09, the period covered by the latest annual report, the RSC sold 532,764 tickets overall, playing to 85 per cent capacity. In Stratford, the company played to 92 per cent capacity at The Courtyard. In addition to the eight plays in The Histories cycle, and a revival of Gregory Doran's production of *A Midsummer Night's Dream*, there were ten productions, of which two were new commissions. The scale of the enterprise, which also includes UK and international touring, and seasons in Newcastle and London, imposes a demanding production cycle on the RSC. It calls for long-term planning and substantial resources in terms of finance, materials, technical skills and creativity.

The complexity of the production cycle and touring are compounded by the fact that offices, workshops, rehearsal rooms and other functions are in different locations spread around Stratford-upon-Avon and London (see figure 1). This imposes not just a geographical but also a psychological and cultural distance between different areas. Moreover, during the period covered in this report, some of the offices and theatre locations were temporary while the new RST was being built.

The RSC's long presence in Stratford-upon-Avon means that it is a significant local employer in a town that is a vital tourist attraction, welcoming three million visitors a year. It has an important relationship with the local community, who monitor the RSC closely. During the period of partial demolition and transformation, the old RST building and the Swan Theatre have been a material reminder of change, evoking complex emotions as a result. The redevelopment represents progress and activity, but also the (temporary) loss of an icon.

As well as operating across different geographic locations, different parts of the organisation are at their busiest at different times of the day. Cleaners and maintenance start early, administrative staff work mainly office hours, others such as front of house staff and technicians have to support matinée and evening performances, and undertake regular weekend work. Many staff and all senior managers have open-ended working time contracts (to a maximum of 48 hours a week averaged over a year). Actors have their own timetables of rehearsals and performances. For everyone, there can be irregular and long hours to meet the needs of specific shows, and the European Working Time Directive has reduced the flexibility of working hours, making operations more complex.

Organisational ageing

In 2003 the RSC had an unusually large number of staff with long tenure, some with over 30 years' service. This brought a strong sense of loyalty and community, but an adherence to traditional practices and values by some staff did not always contribute to the creation of a highly integrated organisation.

The longevity of both staff and organisation meant that there were established networks of staff and areas of authority that, although highly efficient in terms of fulfilling their specific function, concentrated organisational power in certain individuals, who retained certain ways of working. The downside of the positive 'family feeling' was that members of staff expected the organisation to be indulgent and forgiving, and there was an inherent resistance to change.

In addition, as the work of the organisation changed and expanded, the RSC needed to create new functions not previously associated with theatre practice, for example in IT, education and digital media. This brought new people with new skills and different expectations into the organisation.

Summary: the challenges facing the new leadership of the RSC in 2003

A combination of internal and external circumstances created an extremely challenging situation for the new leadership of the RSC in 2003. Attempted change had not been successful, producing internal resistance, weak organisational inter-connectedness, inefficiency and a lack of internal resilience. The new Artistic Director, Michael Boyd, and new Executive Director, Vikki Heywood, faced the following challenges:

Figure 1   RSC locations in the UK

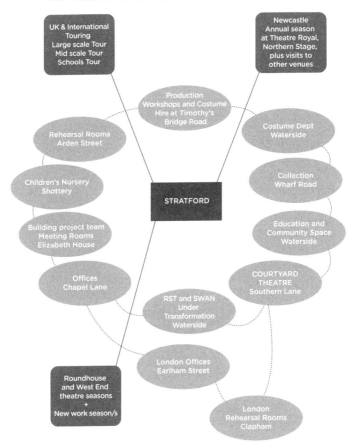

- how to rebuild the morale of the organisation.
- how to rebuild the critical reputation of the RSC, which was low.
- how to restore the confidence of senior management.
- how to restore confidence in senior management.
- how to restore relations with supporters, sponsors and funders, especially the Arts Council.
- how to deal with a looming financial deficit.
- how to handle the loss of a permanently available London theatre
- how to manage the reconstruction of the RST, for which the Arts Council had set aside £50 million in Lottery funding, but which would cost more than double that.
- how to solve the long-term structural problems of the RSC, and rebuild an organisation, while working with the grain of its dominant culture.
- how to do all these things, and continue to show artistic leadership by mounting critically successful productions.

Financially and, more importantly, creatively, the RSC has not only survived the crisis of 1999–2002, but has also re-established its reputation, and is about to open a reconstructed main theatre in Stratford-upon-Avon which physically embodies the ensemble principles discussed in this report. This achievement has happened because of a process of change and growth across the whole organisation that is rooted in the concept of 'ensemble'.

2   Ensemble

I want to say that the ensemble... is the meat and potatoes of what we as actors do.[7]

Actor Sam West, The Stage, 2002

To address the challenges set out in chapter 2, the new leadership of the RSC used the concept of 'ensemble' to bring about change across the whole organisation, not just within the acting company. This chapter explains what ensemble means, the logic of its use at the RSC, and what it was intended to accomplish. It considers the social changes that encourage a more ensemble approach to managing organisations, and identifies a crucial paradox that has to be resolved if the ensemble principle is to become an organisation-wide practice, as opposed to an ideal in the minds of its leaders.

In the RSC's current statement of its 'Purpose and Values' it makes a commitment: 'To create our work through the ensemble principles of collaboration, trust, mutual respect, and a belief that the whole is greater than the sum of its parts'. This purpose should not only govern work on the stage and in the rehearsal room, but extend throughout the operations of the RSC, so as: 'to inspire artists and staff to learn and make theatre at the same time'.[8]

At the RSC, the resuscitation of the ensemble principle from 2002 was, in a sense, a case of 'back to the future'. The word held rhetorical power, and carried with it an appeal both to the organisation's historic achievements and the distinct world of the theatre. As Boyd told the board in 2003:

*The RSC's best and most celebrated work has invariably been the
fruit of an ensemble company of actors, who have developed a
deepened understanding of each other and their material over
a sustained period of time, in an atmosphere of trust, and a
climate of courage.*[9]

Boyd's decision to revive the ensemble principle not only
gave the RSC and its stakeholders' confidence by signalling
continuity within change. In addition, the word has a useful
ambiguity. As Boyd remarked at a meeting that we observed in
February 2007:

*It is a bin that anything could go in. My ideal ensemble is both
closed and monastic, and focused and a whorehouse, and looking out.*

What does ensemble mean?

Ensemble is a French word meaning 'together' or 'viewed as
a whole'. In its simplest theatrical context, ensemble means
no more than a group of actors working together on a
series of productions over time. When it comes to applying
the term more broadly to organisational development,
ensemble should be thought of not only as a way of doing
or as a management tool, but as a way of being, based on a
set of moral principles that guide leadership decisions and
administrative actions. The word may be usefully ambiguous,
but there is no doubt about the values that shape Boyd's
approach. One of his most crafted statements on the topic
was made in a speech given at the New York Public Library
on 20 June 2008. The presentation linked theatrical practice
with organisational form, in the context of social and
cultural changes in the world as a whole:

*Our dominant, secular, western culture is obsessed with
individualism. It is fearful of the boredom, humiliation and
disappointments of collective activity. Just do it yourself, get on with
it yourself and at least you can control the experience you're going
to have. Don't throw yourself at the mercy of other people.*[10]

Boyd argued that at the heart of healthy, creative theatre making is collaboration. But there is a tendency for the open world of theatre to become a closed system, as directors, writers, and designers impose patterns that the actors are then constrained to work to. However, political, social and cultural changes suggest that the spirit of ensemble that is intended to inform the RSC may once more be in tune with the times:

We have found that this approach to theatre making both enables and requires a set of behaviours... worth looking at, because they create our conditions – what we call the conditions for creativity. And they also create the conditions for community. [11]

These behaviours – in the terms of this report, the moral values of ensemble – Boyd summarised as:

Cooperation *The intense and unobstructed traffic between artists at play, that also surrenders to the connection with others even while making demands on ourselves.*

Altruism *The moral imagination and the social perception to see that the whole is greater than the sum of its parts. It is about the stronger helping the weaker, not the weaker being choreographed to make the stronger look good.*

Trust *Otherwise you are not going to be able to experiment or be honest without fear.*

Empathetic curiosity *Caring for others with a forensic curiosity that seeks new ways of being together and creating together.*

Imagination *And time for that imagination, so that we can keep ideas in the mind long enough to allow them to emerge from the alchemy of the imagination rather than the factory of the will.*

Compassion *Engaging with the world and each other, knowing that there may well be mutual pain in doing so.*

Tolerance and forgiveness *To allow mistakes and recover from very big mistakes.*

Humility *The person who has nothing to learn is certainly incapable of creative dialogue.*

Magnanimity *The courage to give away your ideas.*

Love *The ability to be inspired by your whole self and by the whole self of others.*

Rapport *The magic language between individuals in tune with each other.*

Patience *Only really possible and only really called upon in a company that stays together this long... Patience to develop relationships with each other as fellow artists ... The patience to stalk the big beast and achieve what only we can achieve.*

Diversity *Far from imposing homogeneity, a true ensemble requires dynamic difference.*

Boyd added that not everyone in the RSC was expected to display every one of these qualities all the time. These values, he said 'were a report of findings, not a code of behaviour'. They were an ideal, a guiding star by which people could coordinate their individual contribution to the direction taken by the larger whole.

The most formal statement of these values in the company's official papers is in the RSC's first-ever strategic plan, issued in August 2006, which declared:

The values that define the RSC's approach to ensemble are:

· *a commitment to the unexpected, born out of trust and the time the company spends together*

· *a belief that the whole is greater than the sum of its parts*

· *a rigorous approach to training*

· *a duty to experiment*

· *a celebration and nurturing of the skills of emerging artists*

· *creative communication across theatre disciplines*

· *curiosity for and engagement with best practices from other cultures and disciplines.*[12]

Since then the company has summarised these values as being 'collaborative', 'engaging', 'ambitious' and 'enquiring'. Its stated aims are:

· to connect people with Shakespeare
· to engage with the world
· and to work through the principles of ensemble.

Ensemble in the theatre and the acting company

From the beginning, the RSC was conceived as an 'ensemble company'. It was established with the principle of offering long term contracts not only to create the circumstances in which actors could develop their performance skills, but also to generate mutual trust and knowledge that would enhance the work on the stage. While not in any way achieved through an egalitarian process, ensemble productions call for a much stronger sense of co-ownership of creative decisions and they produce a form of social capital.

In our interviews, we noted that many long-serving members of staff referred to the RSC as a 'family', and the RSC has by and large always enjoyed very strong loyalty from its staff. But an ensemble is not a family. Indeed, one generally unacknowledged aspect of the belief in the value of ensemble that presents a strategic challenge to the RSC, is that, although the plays of Shakespeare were written for a 'family' of players, they were not written for an ensemble. Unlike the plays of, for instance, Chekhov or Ibsen, where there is a roughly equal distribution of parts, in the case of Shakespeare there are two or three strong, usually male, leads, some minor character parts, and then a flexible number of one-liners or walk-ons. In addition, there will always be a tension between the theatrical economy's need for 'stars' as lead players and the more communitarian idea of an ensemble where actors play both minor and major parts. The RSC's repertory system also calls for actors to be ready to understudy roles of all sizes and, in the past, leading actors have been reluctant to do this.

During Boyd's tenure, ensemble has been thoroughly re-embedded in the RSC's theatre practice. Early progress was made towards establishing three-year contracts for actors. In the spring of 2006, Boyd began rehearsing a new cycle of Shakespeare's history plays, which he described as: 'the birth of our first two and a half year ensemble... a model of how we would like to produce work in the future'.[13]

Alongside the long contracts, Boyd initiated the 'Artist Development Programme', which required that all actors with the company undertake training and development in everything from voice and verse to rhetoric and movement as a normal part of the working week. Understudying became a requirement – with their agreement – for all actors, regardless of the seniority of their roles or experience.

Nonetheless, the RSC continued to hire stars. Soon after The Histories, the Hamlet ensemble featured David Tennant and Patrick Stewart. In Boyd's words: 'There was no bigger star-led phenomenon.'[14] Casting them tested the resilience of the values of ensemble. It required the ensemble to accommodate stars, and also that the stars themselves fit within the ensemble. Boyd emphasised the latter and the significance that both actors had grown up in the ensemble tradition of the RSC.[15]

In January 2009 rehearsals began with a new ensemble acting company, comprising 44 actors, who would present seven Shakespeare plays and seven other productions over a period of three years. Known informally as the 'Long Ensemble', 17 of the actors had worked at the RSC before, 7 played in The Histories, and 27 were new to the company. The oldest actor was 66, the youngest 22, and 12 were women. The company as a whole encompasses a diverse range of experience, education, accent and ethnic origin.

Extending ensemble to the whole company

From the beginning Boyd made it clear, as he told the board shortly after his appointment, that he believed that ensemble work was the organisation's destiny. He also argued that the organisation as a whole should become more of an ensemble, by breaking down the walls between operational staff and artists, and between the cultures of managers and artists. This prescription flowed from Boyd's analysis of the problems that the RSC had recently faced, including the observations that:

· *There has been an over-specialisation between conception and execution, between artist and manager; and*

· *There has been poor communication between theatre artists and 'members of staff'.*[16]

The board agreed that Boyd's vision needed to be transmitted throughout the organisation and supported by actions that would instil values with which everyone could identify. The means of transmission was to be the Steering Committee, a group of senior managers originally established by Boyd when the previous Managing Director was still in post, but which was now to be the means by which leadership could be distributed beyond the Artistic and Executive

Director. Although at this stage Boyd and the staff were still feeling their way towards the ensemble ideal, in his contribution to the 2004/05 annual report Boyd wrote that ensemble:

Is the way to lift everyone to new and unexpected levels of vividness and clarity. It does not preclude one-part offers, or short contracts, but does demand an understanding and a commitment to the philosophy.

Importantly he went on:

Ensemble is not just about actors. Already we have been investing in training and developing opportunities for assistant directors, costume makers, designers and workshop craftspeople. We need training and development to extend to all staff. [17]

As a signifier of change, and recommitment to purpose, Boyd took the unusual step of opening up the RSC to outside influences by inviting different national and international theatre companies to share in mounting a festival of the complete works of Shakespeare, The Complete Works festival, which ran at Stratford-upon-Avon from April 2006 to March 2007. The experience of working with outside companies, some good, some bad, was a challenge to the RSC's ways of working, but it served to root the changes being made throughout the administration and support operations in the practice of the theatre, grounding wider change in the reality of production and performance.

Ensemble: a moving target

The Complete Works festival and The Histories that followed (alongside productions by other directors) are reminders that the RSC works to an organisational rhythm as new seasons are planned and prepared, new acting companies formed, and new challenges undertaken. These challenges, such as The Complete Works, generate a pulse of pressure points that are often exhausting, but which move the company forward. As the cycle continues, the work of refining the RSC's values and practices goes on. The all-embracing term 'ensemble' turns out to be a moving target, as understanding of its meaning and ways of achieving it change and are refined. Certain actions, not necessarily performed with ensemble in mind, will be seen in chapter 3 to have contributed to the RSC's purpose. Change has to be understood as a developmental process rather than a predetermined plan, an incremental approach achieved by small steps whose full significance often appears only in retrospect.

Ensemble and collaboration: placing the RSC in a wider context

In his speech at the New York Public Library, Boyd spoke of ensemble being increasingly in tune with the zeitgeist. Looking beyond the RSC, it is clear that a number of social, technological and economic factors have interacted to create a climate where the ideas and practice of collaboration have spread across different sectors. It is against this backdrop that the RSC has implemented and been able to implement ensemble.

In their book *The Support Economy*, Harvard Business School Professor Shoshana Zuboff and her husband Dr James Maxmin, chart how processes of production and consumption are increasingly becoming collaborative ventures.[18] Rather than deciding upon an a priori product or service, and then delivering it, organisations are starting from the needs of their customers and then designing ways to meet those needs – increasingly with the customer's collaboration. Similarly, in the realm of public services, there is increasing interest in the co-production of public services between providers and users.[19]

Collaboration is also a major organising principle of the internet. Much software now enables collaborative ventures to happen, such as the online encyclopedia, Wikipedia. Other web 'events', including the success of particular Youtube uploads or 'crowd-sourcing' (the process by which solutions are found to given problems by making an open call to a number of people or a community), occur through the aggregation of individual decisions in an unorganised, but ultimately integrated, fashion.[20]

The point to note about collaboration is that it is motivated by a desire to improve the product, service or outcome for *everyone* who participates or is affected by the collaboration. In the collaborative model, the input of the 'consumer' is assumed to improve the product of the 'producer' and to lead to a better outcome for both. At the RSC this means that organisational change through ensemble should benefit actors, the wider company, the audience, and the 'product' itself. This principle underlies the physical redesign of the RST.

Since audiences are increasingly able to participate in determining their desired outcomes in the commercial and public service arenas, they are likely to demand the opportunity to do the same in the arts sector. As Boyd put it in his New York speech:

The time might be ripe for theatre to offer a better, more honest, more active and intimate relationship also between the performer and the audience. I sense a new contract being drawn up among young theatre-artists... and audiences that acknowledges the audience as part of this ensemble as well.[21]

This is observable in the performance style of the RSC, exploited to the full on the thrust stage, discussed in chapter 3.

Ensemble leadership: a paradox

In an interview for this report, the RSC's founding Artistic Director Sir Peter Hall said that the objectives of ensemble were 'growth, security, confidence, continuity' and, in his view, the words 'ensemble' and 'family' were interchangeable. But that did not mean that the rehearsal process, and still less the running of the company, was egalitarian. He was prepared to describe his own approach as autocratic, and added: 'I don't believe it is possible to run a family, a tribe, or a collective, or whatever, without there being a boss.'[22]

The difficulty of striking a balance between the shared exploratory process in the rehearsal room and the imperative of being on budget and on schedule quickly became apparent in the course of our research. This is the ensemble paradox – that collective creativity nonetheless needs a defining vision and decisive leadership. There is a further paradoxical relationship between the practice of ensemble as a creative and administrative process, and the fact that the RSC is judged by its product: what ends up on stage. The key paradox, however, is that although the values of ensemble have to be held in common in order to succeed, the process of instilling those values throughout the organisation was initiated from the top down. The key to this process was for as many senior managers as possible to take responsibility for its development, as will be seen in chapter 3, where the Steering Committee and a larger Steering Group are discussed in more detail.

In conversations with us, Vikki Heywood, the RSC's Executive Director, acknowledged the paradox inherent in having to 'lead' an ensemble. The RSC, she told us, has to have a visionary Artistic Director but: 'the challenge then is to take that from an autocracy to an empowered group of people all working together to develop a vision'.[23]

The challenge of ensemble leadership, then, is to align the achievement of strategic and operational goals with the organic development of a cooperative and empowered organisational culture. This is the subject of the following chapter.

3   Actions to promote ensemble

In this chapter we list the specific actions taken from 2002 onwards to re-establish the ensemble principle and which contributed to the process of spreading it outwards from the rehearsal room and the acting company to the organisation as a whole.

In setting out what the RSC did to promote the values of ensemble, and to change its practices and procedures, there is a danger of imposing too much retrospective logic. The process was less linear than a list of 'inputs' implies, and, in fact, combined:

- conscious interventions, including introducing external help to facilitate the change process
- leadership in the form of leading by example, providing rhetoric that reflected the organisation's emerging narrative back to itself, and decision-making
- self-organisation in the form of organic change at individual, team and departmental level
- experimentation that sometimes resulted in setbacks, failure and frustration.

Nevertheless, the change process to date can be seen as happening within three main chronological blocks. It starts with the appointment of new leaders who decide on the need for organisational development and begin to make changes to behaviour, structures and practices. It continues with the decision to work with an external advisor and facilitator, and to have the process observed by external researchers, thereby making a public commitment to intervention and organisation-wide change. And the third stage, a significant mark of confidence, is to take control of the change process through internal direction and a commitment to organic growth.

We have identified these overlapping periods as three stages in a continuing process:

· preparation
· mobilisation
· integration

Embedding ensemble throughout the whole organisation has not been, and perhaps never can be, completed. The next stage, consolidation, will involve continuing to increase the self-organising capabilities of middle management and staff, and the company is already examining ways in which to extend the ensemble principle to include its audiences as well.

Preparation

In 2001, a new governance and board structure had been formed, under the new chairmanship of Lord Alexander, with his predecessor, Sir Geoffrey Cass, as Vice-President. In June 2004, Sir Christopher Bland was invited by the board to succeed Lord Alexander as Chairman. The process of reconstructing and reconfiguring the RSC's senior management team had already begun. Vikki Heywood, who had just successfully overseen the rebuilding and re-opening of the Royal Court Theatre in London, joined as Interim Managing Director in September 2003, and was subsequently offered a permanent post, under the new title Executive Director. This title was felt to reflect more accurately the relationship with the Artistic Director, and the post's administrative responsibilities. While Boyd leads the RSC as Artistic Director, Heywood works closely with him in a 'duumvirate', and both are RSC board members.

Sir Christopher Bland told us that, at first, he was sceptical about the wisdom of the RSC being run by Boyd and Heywood as a duumvirate: 'All organisational manuals tell you that it will not work.' However, he now sees the chairman's role as being to glue the partnership of Boyd and Heywood together, 'not that it really ever comes unstuck'.[24] In his view, the duumvirate averts the potential problems caused by having either an Artistic Director who is not interested in finance, or a Chief Executive who is not interested in the creative work. Bland explained the importance of Boyd and Heywood's partnership to the formulation of an ensemble vision for the RSC:

Michael Boyd would have thought [in 2002] that it [ensemble] was an acting concept. With his support, Vikki Heywood has extended it to the organisation. She has enhanced his understanding of the concept.[25]

Bland described himself as overseeing a work in progress and an evolution, rather than a pre-determined programme of change.

Further changes were made at senior levels of the organisation. Andrew Parker, who had previously worked for an international publishing company and who had been a consultant on the RSC's management restructure and served in an interim capacity, became Director of Finance and Administration in July 2004, with reporting responsibilities to the board.

Management structure
In order to improve communications, and reduce the hierarchical nature of the administration, a broad-based management structure was introduced.

Steering Committee In an unprecedented step for the organisation, Boyd extended the senior management team from a close-knit cartel of three to a much larger group of 12 all with equal say and equal status. Along with the executive trio of Artistic and Executive Directors and the Director of Finance and Administration, this group formed the new, expanded and more distributed senior management of the RSC. When we began this research, its membership had been further expanded to 18 senior managers from a range of core departments, meeting weekly.

Steering Group This has a much larger membership, and combines members of the Steering Committee with less senior managers, principally heads of departments. It meets monthly and, in January 2007, had 55 members. The purpose of Steering Group is 'to refine policy and feed back input from across the organisation'.[26]

Boyd describes Steering Group as being operational and Steering Committee as being strategic. Heywood has been concerned to ensure that both Steering Committee and Steering Group take ownership of the change process by having responsibility for specific aspects, such as the development of inter-departmental working. The intention is to distribute leadership throughout the organisation.

While this process was under way, members of the RSC board began to take responsibility for policy areas relating to their own particular expertise, for example, fundraising, education or marketing – and to work closely with the appropriate members of the RSC staff. The effect of this was to integrate board members more with the organisation and bring board members closer to executive decisions of the RSC. Heywood had been conscious of the distance between the board and the rest of the organisation: 'On this journey, we need to bring them in, because they need to understand why we are moving towards this model'.[27]

Other steps taken to address this included a board and staff away day and opportunities for board members to observe management meetings. Board members are also actively involved in the building project for the new RST.

General recruitment

As opportunities arose, and the ensemble principle became established as an organisational idea, recruitment decisions were made on the basis of 'people skills' as well as craft and technical experience. Candidates were interviewed with ensemble in mind. In describing the interview process, one recruit said:

Ensemble was mentioned inasmuch as I couldn't avoid it... from the advert up to the moment I accepted the job; it was fairly high up the agenda as a key message.

Ensemble also came to play a part in the arrival of new recruits to the organisation. As part of the change process, induction became more formalised and expectations of new members of the organisation were made clearer. In 2009, Chris McGill, a member of The Histories ensemble, was commissioned to produce a short induction film, *Welcome to the RSC*. It features introductions to the RSC and its work, both organisational and artistic, by Heywood and Boyd, the latter speaking in detail about the RSC as a 'learning organisation'. Welcoming packs, including a DVD featuring the documentary, are now sent to all staff and actors before they start with the organisation. The pack includes a detailed description of who's who in the RSC and different departmental responsibilities, a copy of the latest RSC newsletter *Omnibus*, and details of the RSC's education work.

Artistic Planning

In addition to the management structure described above, there is a further high-level committee, Artistic Planning. As the name implies, it is devoted to the development of the RSC's theatrical programme and makes decisions about what plays will be presented and by whom they will be directed, designed and performed. Although the decisions taken by Artistic Planning affect all aspects of the organisation, prior to 2003 it was a small, closed group that was regarded as both exclusive and secretive.

In 2003, however, Boyd, in a radical move, expanded the membership of Artistic Planning to include the Education, Marketing, Sales, Finance, Executive, Fundraising, Commercial and Technical departments alongside the traditional artistic domains of Producers, Associate Directors, Casting, Literary and Voice. In 2007, Artistic Planning was extended further to include Estates, Human Resources, Development, General Counsel and Communications. This more open process has allowed for more effective planning and organisational integration. It puts theatre at the heart of the organisation, and organisational considerations at the heart of Artistic Planning.

Basic functional improvements

One senior member of staff, involved in strategic decisions during the restructuring of the organisation, commented to us that the first things to be done were obvious:

There wasn't a management team and the work was clearly defined by roles and levels of authority... There was a lot to do to establish financial management, delegate authority and improve qualities of communication.

Some basic steps addressed these issues. Some of the earliest were taken in relation to financial management.

In 2003 responsibility for both departmental budgets and management was devolved to heads of departments, with the effect that by 2005 there were 'around 80 budget holders' in the organisation.[28] Later, the finance team regularly gave training to managers, and the Finance Director visited departments to explain financial procedures and how they fitted into the wider context of the RSC's accounts.

Another change was that the 'flattening' of hierarchy seen at senior levels in the early years of Boyd and Heywood's leadership was continued throughout the organisation: during the period of our research, membership of Steering Group grew from 55 in January 2007, to 66 in June 2009. Additions included middle managers from Human Resources, Production and Education. The remit of Steering Group also grew as Boyd, Heywood and others opened more areas of the organisation's business to discussion at that level.

Physical re-organisation

The decision to remodel the Royal Shakespeare Theatre in Stratford-upon-Avon was in itself both a cause and a reflection of significant change. By designing both the temporary Courtyard Theatre and the new RST around the principle of a thrust stage, the mental and physical barrier created by a proscenium arch separating actors and audience is eliminated. Both are 'in the same room', and the use of a thrust stage brings all seats into much closer proximity with the performance area. The maximum distance between audience member and the stage has been reduced from 27 to 15 metres. Similarly, the circulation spaces within the RST have been reconfigured to enlarge the possibilities of social interaction, including a seven-day-a-week events and exhibition programme.

In the summer of 2007, a new block of offices and meeting rooms was opened in Chapel Lane in order to accommodate departments that had lost their home when the old RST was closed. The new building's design was developed in accordance with the values of ensemble. Several departments that had been separate were brought together under the same roof, and the offices of senior managers were spread around the building. Instead of being brick-walled, as at the old RST, they are glazed and transparent. The majority of the staff sits in an open plan arrangement, joining different departments together. Corridor spaces, meeting areas and kitchens have been designed to increase informal contact. The foyer has room for large gatherings – on occasion social – and it also houses a bank of computers with internet access for use by actors, who are thereby given a reason to visit the administrative building. To keep Chapel Lane in touch with the theatre, monitors in the foyer screen live-feeds of the stage.

Mobilisation
Having started both a physical and managerial restructuring of the organisation, the next phase was intended to help motivate all members of staff to contribute to the change process by accepting individual responsibility for its implementation.

External support for the change process

In 2006, the RSC engaged an organisational development expert, Dr Mee-Yan Cheung-Judge, to advise the RSC leadership, to work with the internal change team and assist the process of spreading ensemble ideas and working throughout the company, and to facilitate a series of meetings devoted to change management. Together, she and the RSC's leaders planned a series of interventions in the form of meetings directed at opening up thinking within the organisation, finding new directions for the company, and exploring and communicating the values of ensemble.

The key principles agreed were that the change process and interventions should:

- encourage self-determination. The interventions would be directed towards mobilising the organisation to define ensemble for itself, to personalise and internalise its meaning and to increase the capacities of people to take their own decisions. Only in this way could organisational development become a sustainable practice.
- focus on middle management, because unless this group was engaged, change would be unsustainable. Ensemble needed to be co-constructed by this group, not be imposed upon them. Only if this group took ownership of ensemble would it become a true organisational practice.
- make the whole organisation aware of the need for, and the practicalities of change.
- link organisational change to the RSC's high-level strategy, so that people could see why change was necessary.

The appointment of an external advisor was in itself an explicit declaration to the organisation on the part of the RSC leadership that they were investing in organisational development on a scale that was intended to transform the whole organisation.

In January 2008, the change process was broadened to include the entire staff in a series of meetings designed in collaboration with Boyd and Heywood so as to allow the organisation to discuss and determine what it collectively felt ensemble working at the RSC should look like, and how far it had travelled on the journey towards that goal. In order to encourage the participation of all staff, the process took the form of five identically structured half-day sessions involving everyone.

The externally facilitated workshops brought clarity to issues related to the change process and enabled disparate opinions within the RSC to be aired. They also created greater personal and organisational self-awareness and set some practical parameters. At the workshops, the organisation was asked where it collectively thought it was on the process towards becoming ensemble. Groups were asked to position the RSC on a road map, with a fork in the road ahead. The collective judgement was that the RSC had reached the fork, and that it had the potential to turn either way, becoming more or less ensemble. After the workshops, it was agreed that the process of implementing change had to be more fully integrated with Human Resources and more clearly communicated within the organisation. Subsequently, this indeed happened, with Human Resources guiding and communicating the process.

Taking the ensemble principle into the public arena

The ensemble vision of the RSC takes artistic practice as its model. Changes made there set the tone and conditions for organisational change. As the core of the RSC's purpose and activity, the success and response to the artistic work has been a testing ground and vehicle for the ensemble concept itself. As we have seen, one of the first major steps was The Complete Works festival, which opened the relatively closed world of the Stratford-upon-Avon 'campus' to visiting theatre companies with different aesthetics and working methods. This was a major challenge: asking the organisation to accommodate different people and techniques and move swiftly from one production to another.

Members of staff recall the importance of The Complete Works as a turning point:

*We deliberately blew up the model with The Complete Works,
and now we must continue on this journey of co-production,
international awareness and multiculturalism... It can't go back.*

From an actor's point of view:

*When I had first arrived in Stratford in the winter of 1999...
it could not have been more different. Morale was low and, I
couldn't believe it, but actors just didn't want to be there. Now, the
place was humming and it felt like the Edinburgh Festival with
so many people from all over the world performing, watching,
playing and enjoying.*[29]

Steps were also taken to open acting companies and
the creative work up to the audience. The most fundamental
decision was to alter and improve the physical relationship
between audience and actors. The use of a thrust stage
has produced a significant change in the relationship
between players and the audience. It both extends and
is complemented by Boyd's directorial style, in which he
frequently asks actors to involve the audience, and in which
characters either appear in or speak from different parts of
the auditorium.

The actors continued this ethos of inclusion and
reaching out as they began to engage more deeply in the
educational work of the organisation (see chapter 4) and to
work with amateur dramatic groups. Similarly, during The
Histories, actors began to write blogs for the general public,
describing life in the company. Actor Nick Asbury's blog was
subsequently published as a book in 2009.

The process of developing the new RST has been
central to the organisation's integration with its public.
The designs for the new RST, with the specific aspects
that embody the ensemble values described earlier, were
made public, and its spaces have been planned so that the
organisation and the public will come into greater contact
with each other.

Reconfiguring the role of Human Resources

On her appointment as Director of Human Resources in 2005, Adele Cope set out to re-establish the department as an integrated, and more benign, function. In 2010, she described the challenges that she faced:

Beforehand there was an HR department that was asked to be quite different in its approach. I'm used to a much more advisory service of empowering managers to make their own decisions and to do so safely. So they probably took a fair amount of time to trust me, because they were used to coming in and being told what to do. Instead they'd come in to see me and I'd ask them what they'd like to do, and then we'd talk about how that could be achieved and if it was possible. So they became part of the decision making process, and that's very much the approach that I've taken, which I think also fits with the way the organisation wants to go.

Cope repositioned Human Resources as an advisory function and a 'go-to' department, empowering managers and repositioning them as accountable for management decisions. Specific appointments, such as the Training and Development Manager, were made to develop the capacity.

Improved organisation-wide communication and discussion

At the RSC, Human Resources covers many things beyond the formal management of people. Along with the Communications Department, led by Liz Thompson, Cope and her team have taken responsibility for many of the structural and everyday aspects of ensemble. General communication and information is conveyed via the weekly electronic and paper newsletter *Omnibus*, which is created by the Communications team, which manages a range of other internal communications channels. Human Resources and others have encouraged Steering Group members to use regular departmental meetings to communicate relevant information to those whom they manage.

Prior to Boyd and Heywood's leadership of the RSC, there had been little opportunity for the staff to come together to debate issues of concern to them and have input into the direction that the organisation followed. There were occasional Full Company Meetings in which announcements were made, but these were ad hoc. Boyd and Heywood introduced a more regular structure for large-scale meetings. Three times a year there are full Staff Meetings that include actors. Importantly, Boyd and Heywood do not run these meetings as 'talking heads', imparting decisions and strategy to the organisation; rather, they run them as debates in which all are able to participate. Over and above these meetings, there are Staff Forums and Actor's Forums in which groups can debate issues amongst themselves. Full company meetings continue but are used on a very pragmatic and functional basis, for instance, to inform the entire organisation of press announcements of forthcoming seasons. As Heywood later explained to us, these changes were made with the intention of providing many more ways in which people can meet either departmentally or cross-departmentally, and allow ideas to be captured for the benefit of the organisation.

Beyond the communication of general information, however, Boyd, Heywood and other members of the leadership team also opened the values and motivation behind the change process to discussion. Specific developments were discussed at Steering Group level, exposing them to deliberation by heads of departments, managers and others responsible for their communication within the organisation.

Increased cross-departmental working
As part of the change process, greater emphasis was placed – particularly by Human Resources – on specific projects that would bring different departments that might not otherwise work together into closer working relationships:

- Discussions in Steering Group raised awareness of issues that affected behaviour across all departments. Specifically, these were recruitment and selection, management and team development, meeting structure and appraisals. Working groups were established, drawing together members of

Steering Group from different departments to discuss these
issues and make recommendations to the next Group meeting.
· The RSC began to use Tessitura, an integrated customer
database for fundraising, membership, ticketing and marketing.
The effect was to create a single system used by several different
departments. Tessitura is itself a system that is continuously
developed by its subscribers in the cultural sector.
· Departmental 'meet and greets' also occur. Representatives
of different departments either invite others to see what they
do or visit meetings in other areas to explain their work.
For instance, theatre directors from the artistic side of the
organisation visited the IT department's away day.

Integration

Having begun the process of change, it was necessary for the
RSC to embed the ensemble principle by securing a permanent
shift in the ethos of the organisation and establishing ensemble
as 'a way of being'.

Becoming a learning organisation

Human Resources took the lead in helping the RSC to become
a 'learning organisation'. Learning is at the heart of Boyd's
vision for the RSC: 'if you are not learning, you cannot make
art', he told the board and Steering Committee in September
2008. This was both formal – connecting members of staff
to training programmes – and also informal, as Human
Resources initiated and coordinated the 'Ensemble Learning
Programme' in which members of the RSC can teach each
other skills that can be either professional, such as IT skills and
understanding company finance or general, for instance classes
in Shakespeare, gardening, rhetoric and public speaking.

Learning has now become part of the ethos of the
organisation. Specific departments, such as Voice and
Movement, have traditionally offered training beyond the
acting company but new schemes were also put in place
for all staff. Learning and the enhanced communication of
information and knowledge within the organisation went

hand in hand. A programme of work shadowing has been introduced. For instance, front of house Manager, James Kitto, shadowed Vikki Heywood. Heywood herself shadowed the Costume Department during *Julius Caesar* in 2009. Over the course of 2008/09, more than 80 members of staff shadowed each other in this way and more are scheduled to do so in the future. Learning opportunities are also themed around productions: during the 2009 Russian season, Russian language classes were made available and lectures for the acting company were opened up to other members of staff.

Leadership training

In order to improve standards of leadership throughout the organisation, the decision was taken to offer all members of Steering Group who wished to do so the opportunity to take part in the leadership training schemes set up by the national Cultural Leadership Programme. To date, 24 managers from the RSC have attended the Clore Short Course, an intensive, two-week training course delivered by the Clore Leadership Programme at a cost of around £1,300 per attendee. A further two managers are to attend a similar course in March 2010. The training represents a significant investment of time and money by the RSC, and attendees have been keen to apply the lessons learned.

Education

In addition to recognising the importance of learning within the organisation, the Education Department took on greater importance in the RSC's public profile. With the Education Department represented in Artistic Planning, programming was connected to the school curriculum and focused on the needs of schools. From The Histories onwards, actors worked directly on teacher training programmes as part of the RSC's national Stand Up for Shakespeare campaign. Some were also supported in undertaking postgraduate teaching awards at the University of Warwick; 25 actors will have qualified by the end of 2010. The RSC took an ensemble approach to these ventures, working with schools as clusters and establishing The

Learning and Performance Network, a network of partnerships across over 300 communities nationwide. The RSC's education work is explored further in chapter 4.

Giving recognition

Ensemble values depend upon recognising the value of others' contributions, and individuals feeling that their own work is valued in return. Changes were made to increase recognition of both individual contribution and organisational achievement:

- The section of the website, 'Behind the scenes', now details the story of how a production is put on, and the contribution of many different departments.
- More departments are represented in managerial groups, such as Artistic Planning, Steering Group and Steering Committee.
- In an unprecedented step, in 2008 recent artistic work began to be discussed at Steering Group level, with board members present: different departments across the organisation, outside what is conventionally thought of as the artistic sphere, were given the opportunity to critique the work on stage.
- The organisation-wide newsletter *Omnibus* includes space in which aspects of organisational life, such as specific contributions to a particular performance, people's birthdays and staff departures, can be mentioned and achievements recognised.

Conviviality

The more structural changes put in place to support ensemble have also been complemented by attempts to encourage an informal sense of togetherness. The open-plan design of Chapel Lane, for instance, was conceived with conversation and communication between people from different departments in mind, but further changes were also made that created opportunities and circumstances through which the organisation could come together. 'Cake Friday' is held monthly and hosted by different departments. It arose from discussions with Heywood in which staff consistently mentioned the need for more social gatherings. The new staff catering facilities for the rebuilt RST have been designed so that as many staff as possible can eat together. There are also twice yearly 'staff night' performances in the theatre. Other occasions for coming together are the RSC choir and informal classes such as yoga.

Web presence

As observed in chapter 2, changes at the RSC coincided with dramatic shifts in attitudes to collaboration and participation in organisations and society more widely. In this way, some of those changes were intended not only to impact upon the workings of the organisation, but simultaneously to find new ways to connect the RSC to its audiences and communities. In common with many organisations in the cultural sector, the RSC responded to online opportunities. A new role, Head of Digital Media, was created within the Communications Department. New sections were added to the website including a feature on ensemble in which each actor is given a profile page, introducing the audience to the actors that they see on stage, and blogs by actors from within most of the RSC's current acting companies including The Histories and onwards. The RSC is also working with Channel 4's 4IP project to create a play using Twitter. In this way, the website is developing from being a tool by which potential audiences can find out about performances and book tickets to becoming an embodiment of ensemble.

Visual identity

Change was also marked by a new visual identity implemented by the Marketing Department in 2004. The RSC's new colour scheme of red was applied, from the bars and seats of the Courtyard and the offices at Chapel Lane, to the website and the stationery and business cards used throughout the organisation. Walking around the theatres and the streets of Stratford-upon-Avon, it is also evident on company vehicles and as the colour of sweatshirts worn by employees. In response to audience feedback, front of house staff have adopted a standard uniform that is much more informal. The transformation of the RSC's appearance is echoed in the way in which members of staff interact with the public. The redesign of posters, programmes and website combine to convey the message that the RSC is an ensemble organisation.

Leadership style

Boyd and Heywood adopted and developed a leadership style that established the ethos of ensemble working. Boyd dispensed with perks such as a chauffeured car, and a stricter and more equal expenses policy was introduced. People also took on leadership roles for themselves. For instance, as the members of the wider Steering Committee took greater strategic ownership of their respective areas of operation, they changed their behaviours accordingly. This was fundamental to the success of the project. Later, through workshops facilitated by Dr Mee-Yan Cheung-Judge, this principle of taking on leadership was spread out to Steering Group.

When the new administrative offices were created at Chapel Lane, Boyd and Heywood chose offices at either end of an open plan area so that they had to walk through a 'pool' of staff in order to meet each other; equally, staff would not have to go to a focused, area of power' to meet them.

Boyd and Heywood took care to be approachable and always available to staff. One incoming member of the organisation remarked that in his previous job:

There was a vast gap between me, and the director... Here, there's no barrier between me and Vikki and Michael, and certainly no problem saying 'I'd like a quick chat with Vikki', which would have been unthinkable with the director [in my previous organisation].

In particular, the Human Resources and Communications teams were careful to communicate the change programme with a light touch. Where possible, change was made manifest through actions rather than instilled in a publicly branded initiative.

Looking outwards

As well as addressing the RSC's internal organisation, the concept of ensemble has helped it to look outwards and to play a role in the local, regional and national community. The RSC has sought to establish good relations with the people of Stratford, and strengthen links with the West Midlands in general. This has meant that the RSC has come to be seen as a local partner and a local contributor, helping to influence local transport policy and regional development, working both with neighbouring arts organisations and local businesses. The RSC also has a national role as a leading arts organisation, seeking to influence government arts, education and economic policies, and taking a lead in the Cultural Olympiad as part of the London 2012 Olympic Games.

4 Evidence of progress

In this chapter we look at the changes that resulted from actions taken since 2002, and observe how they affected the process of re-establishing the ensemble principle. In terms of the output of the RSC – the work on stage – the change process has had a markedly positive effect. However, a significant methodological problem for us and the RSC, was how the complex, existential process of becoming an ensemble organisation could be assessed in objective terms. Objective outcomes are apparent in external metrics such as box office receipts, financial returns and critical response. Other outcomes are harder to assess because they are emotional and behavioural. We charted these less easily assessed changes in our observations and interviews. We also made two comparative network analyses in the summers of 2007 and 2009.

Measurement

Following the initial internal exploration in 2007 of the values and intentions, the issue arose of how progress could be measured. The commissioning of this report provided one, external, means of monitoring progress towards becoming an ensemble organisation.

In June 2008, after analysing feedback from the workshops in January, a Steering Group workshop was held to discuss what criteria should be used to determine how far the organisation had progressed towards becoming an ensemble. The facilitator recommended putting in place a series of metrics called a 'dashboard' consisting of milestones and benchmarks by which the organisation could gauge its progress and hold itself accountable. This measurement process would also set a target date by which ensemble working should be achieved.

The response to these proposals about measurement was significant. The RSC held back on setting targets and imposing deadlines because it conflicted with the organic perception of ensemble as a 'way of being' and with Boyd's belief that 'if you know where you are going completely and from the start, it does not work'.[30] It was also thought that metrics in a formal sense ran counter to the RSC's culture and values – 'it was too complicated and corporate' was one comment – and might therefore undermine the change process that it was intended to promote. This 'collective push-back' was taken as a 'sign of confidence' by one interviewee.

On reflection, however, it was agreed that a staff survey might be helpful as a means of evaluating the organisation's progress towards becoming ensemble, and as a gauge of how far through the organisation the values of ensemble and new working practices had spread, as long as the RSC 'owned' the process, and devised the survey in terms that would be meaningful and acceptable to members of staff and the acting company. The staff survey was conducted in the summer of 2009, and its results are discussed in chapter 5.

The RSC's response to the idea of measurement runs counter to the practice of most organisations. Although the organisation has clearly adopted tight and regular measurement in some functions – especially finance, as would be expected – as a whole it has managed to achieve a rapid and significant improvement in its operations, free from the dogma of 1980s and 1990s management theory which maintains that when something cannot be counted, it does not count.

Our own solution to the problem of measurement was to look for evidence of change in three main areas:

- external validation
- internal networking
- cultural change

Evidence of external validation
Critical response to the work on stage

Speaking in February 2009, Sir Christopher Bland observed that 'there is nothing like a successful season to restore the morale of a theatre company, but the converse is also true.'[31]

The critical response to The Histories, and especially The Glorious Moment, when all eight history plays were performed back-to-back, was extremely positive. Among the awards won by the RSC, Boyd was named Best Director by the Theatre Managers' Association (TMA); The Histories won the Special Editor's Award at the Evening Standard Awards 2008 and were named Best Company Performance at the prestigious Olivier Awards of 2009. One review, in particular, was significant. In the *Telegraph,* Charles Spencer wrote:

When Michael Boyd took over the artistic directorship of the RSC, and spoke of restoring the ensemble principle to an organisation that seemed terminally demoralised, I'm afraid I thought, 'Oh yeah, we've heard all this before'.

He continued:

Let me state unreservedly that Boyd's history cycle offers some of the greatest acting, in some of the most imaginative and rigorous productions, that I have experienced in more than 30 years of professional theatre-going.[32]

Spencer's review was of great internal importance to the RSC. For many, it justified their efforts to extend the ensemble principle to the organisation as a whole. Discussing this review a month later, Chris Hill, Director of Sales and Marketing, commented: 'Michael Boyd talks very eloquently about ensemble: now, we have the proof, and therefore we can talk about ensemble more realistically.'[33]

Box office
Box office returns are a tangible indication of a theatre's public success. Figure 2, which is based on available ticket capacity, shows that the RSC sold an increasing percentage of available capacity in Stratford-upon-Avon as the changes we have observed began to take place.

Figure 2   **Percentage of ticket capacity sold, 2002—2009**

■ 2002—09 % Ticket capacity in Stratford-upon-Avon

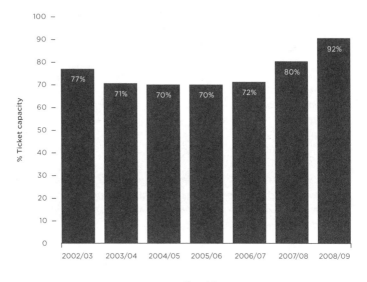

Financial year

Financial progress
Changes in financial management brought about an improvement in the ability of the RSC to manage its finances. The devolution of budgets to individual managers:

· led to increased departmental autonomy
· placed greater responsibility on individual managers

- improved the timely flow and useful content of data
- created a feedback system that was more responsive and easier to correct
- helped achieve a better financial result

According to Andrew Parker, Director of Finance and Administration, devolving budgets helped to generate an operational surplus of £2.4 million in 2003/04 and £1.7 million in 2004/05. The purpose of these surpluses was to contribute to an organisation-wide initiative to eliminate the RSC's accumulated deficit, which was achieved.

The changes in financial management also brought about a change in the attitude and confidence of budget-holders. Parker described the effect on staff, saying: 'At first, there was some resistance to devolved budgets, but now people enjoy the autonomy, and take their accountability very seriously.'[34]

Over the last three years, management accounts show the system bedding down, with variations of actual results from budget decreasing. For the year 2007/08, variations from budget of total income and expenditure were 1 per cent in each case. In 2006/07 they had been 6 per cent and 1 per cent respectively, and in 2005/06, 4 per cent and 4 per cent.

Evidence of internal networking: improved collaboration and internal resilience
Network analysis

As part of our initial survey in 2007, every member of staff we interviewed was asked to complete a network questionnaire about their formal and informal contacts within the organisation: 22 were returned. From these, we developed network diagrams that showed how staff *perceived* different kinds of relationships to exist. We repeated this process in the summer of 2009.

From the dataset of responses, we created six pictures of the organisation that express its constituent relationships in different ways. There are three pairs, comparing 2007 with 2009. Respectively, these examined:

- official working networks: who works directly with whom across the organisation
- informal working networks: who sees whom regularly during their working hours
- social networks: who sees whom in social contexts.

These are illustrated in figures 3 to 8 and were constructed using a software package called UCINET.[35]

The diagrams are included with a number of caveats. Most importantly, the diagrams provide a *general sense and overview at a particular moment in time* of how the organisation works. They are to be looked at largely in relation to their shape: the more compact the clustering and the denser the connecting lines, the stronger the network. UCINET uses data to construct a diagram in terms of pattern, and so the length of connecting lines is *not* a qualitative statement about individual relationships.

The main point to be taken from the diagrams is the contrast between their different overall shapes and the illustration that it provides of the strength of different networks within the RSC. Overall, they provide a visual representation that supports the observations made in the body of this report. In each diagram, white nodes represent people to whom we spoke and from whom we were able to obtain data for the networks. Black nodes represent people for whom time and circumstances meant we were unable to obtain data – they have been filled in using the responses of others.

The networks in operation at the RSC

Official working networks Figures 3 and 4 illustrate the official working networks in operation at the RSC during the summers of 2007 and 2009.

Observations

- The greater density of connecting lines in 2009 suggests that, although there was regular communication between individuals and departments in 2007, this had become even greater during the intervening period.

Figure 3 **Official working network, summer 2007**

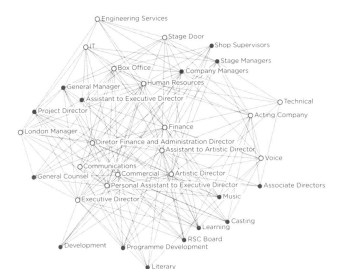

- The overall shape of the network in 2009 is more compact and rounded, suggesting a more even pattern of links than in 2007. A star-shaped pattern would have suggested hierarchy and centralisation. While the 2007 network is reasonably distributed, the close cluster of functions at the centre of the network in 2009 reveals a more evenly balanced pattern of connection.
- The RSC's leadership – the partnership of the Artistic and Executive Directors – is central to each diagram. This, with the distributed pattern of the networks, supports the findings from interviews that the leaders are accepted as necessary within the ensemble ideal. In both 2007 and 2009, the relative positions of Boyd and Heywood in the working networks also reflect their respective responsibilities. The Artistic Director links strongly to the 'creative' side of the organisation, while the Executive Director, like the third member of the senior leadership team – the Director of Finance and Administration – is very well linked to the administrative side. This shows consistent and coherent leadership during the time of our study.

Figure 4   **Official working network, summer 2009**

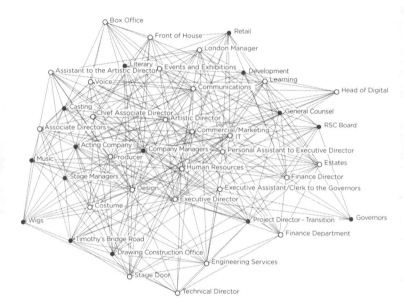

- The commercial operations are noticeably more of a hub in the 2009 network. This reflects a concentration of functions in that area after restructuring, greater representation of commercial activity in areas like Artistic Planning, and cross-departmental working patterns such as that around Tessitura.
- The importance of the assistants to the Artistic and Executive Directors is clear. They are points of connection across the whole organisation. In this light, it is encouraging in relation to the ensemble ideal that the Artistic and Executive Directors themselves remain strongly connected to the organisation as a whole.
- In the 2007 network, there is clear zoning between organisational functions: the artistic side of the RSC clusters on one side (the right in the diagram) and the administrative on the other. In the 2009 network, there are greater and more frequent working connections between the creative

roles and more administrative functions. In particular, the acting company appears less isolated, which could reflect both the timing of our first interviews (at the beginning of The Histories performances in Stratford-upon-Avon) and the increased integration of the acting company within the organisation. The latter interpretation is generally supported by the interviews.

· In each network, departments that are more geographically separated from the main office areas appear at the edge of the diagram. Although they are often as connected to different parts of the RSC as others more centrally located, their connections are with specific areas rather than with the whole.

Informal working networks Figures 5 and 6 represent the informal working networks that existed during the same two periods, the summers of 2007 and 2009.

Observations Informal networks play a vital part in the life and work of modern organisations. According to two authors writing for the *Harvard Business Review*:

The formal organisation is set up to handle easily anticipated problems. But when unexpected problems arise, the informal organisation kicks in. Its complex web of social ties form every time colleagues communicate, and solidify over time into surprisingly stable networks. Highly adaptive, informal networks move diagonally and elliptically, skipping entire functions to get things done.[36]

Informal networks have always played an important part in the RSC and they continue to do so.

· In both figures 5 and 6, the informal working networks are dense and compact. In 2007, we observed the strength of the informal working network (figure 5). Of the three types of networks we analysed (official working, informal working and social), it was the densest, most regular and most compact at the time. This demonstrates the importance

Figure 5 **Informal working network, summer 2007**

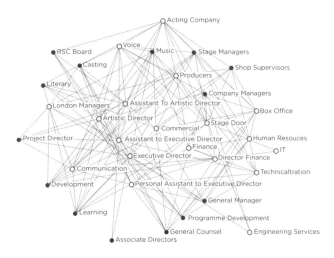

Figure 6 **Informal working network, summer 2009**

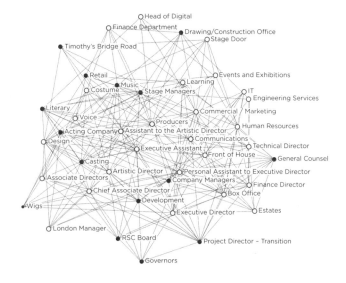

of informal communication in building a common culture and ethos within an organisation and in creating channels of communication that can run alongside, and sometimes bypass, more official channels. In 2007, our analysis revealed an organisation that was to some extent relying upon the resilience provided by informal networks. By 2009, although the informal working network remained strong, it is less markedly different from the formal working network. This implies that the changes made to bring people from different areas of the organisation together were bringing the strength of the informal networks to bear on the working networks at the RSC.

· The leadership team is at the centre of each of the *informal* working networks. This indicates good informal ties between the leadership and the rest of the organisation, and complements evidence from the interviews that both Boyd and Heywood are approachable and accessible.

· As in the official working network, in 2007 and 2009, the assistants to the Artistic and Executive Directors are also central, also suggesting there are good channels of communication and ease of access between the leadership and the rest of the organisation.

· Zoning is apparent in the 2007 network, with the artistic side of the organisation clustered roughly around the top of the diagram, and the administrative side to the left. In the 2009 network, this is less the case, suggesting greater integration. In interviews, the perception of the same respondents was that the organisation was indeed more integrated than it had been in 2007 but that there was still a way to go.

Social networks We have included analysis of the RSC's social networks in 2007 and 2009 for two reasons. First, the social networks shown in figures 7 and 8 provide a control and comparison with the formal and informal working networks. Second, we use them to examine the distinctively social atmosphere that many members of staff, particularly the more long-standing, reported as characteristic of the RSC.

Figure 7   **Social network, summer 2007**

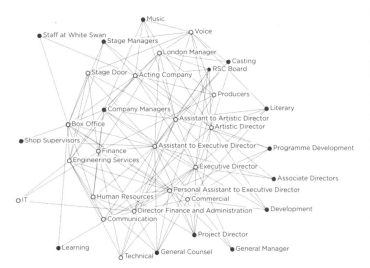

Figure 8   **Social network, summer 2009**

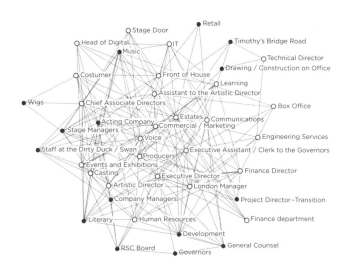

Observations

- As might be expected, in both social networks, points are more dispersed than in the official and informal working networks. This reflects the personal nature of social relationships. Connections are also comparatively fewer and less dense. However, they remain reasonably regular and imply that a strong social network exists around the RSC.
- Compared to the other two networks, the social networks are more star-like in appearance, with more projecting limbs. This emphasises the dense nature of the other diagrams and implies a strong sense of compactness in working relationships around the RSC.
- As with the working and informal working networks, the Artistic and Executive Directors and their assistants are central to social networks. This is an encouraging sign for ensemble working, suggesting that the relationship between leadership and the organisation is consistent throughout the three networks.
- Although there is some zoning, the division between artistic and administrative functions is less apparent than in the previous two networks. This implies a social network that is more mixed than the working networks within the organisation.

Changes in the visualisation of the organisation

In 2007 the RSC conceived of its management structure – as do many organisations – in hierarchical terms. This was expressed as an organogram: 'The simplest possible view of an organisation's reporting structure [that] diagrams both responsibility and channels of communication.'[37]

The organogram (figure 9) shows a clear separation of the artistic and administrative sides of the organisation. Expressed in vertical format, it also gave visual precedence to the senior management team.

In 2008 the RSC developed a new way of visualising its organisation. Although different areas of responsibility are still apparent – the Artistic and Executive Directors remain

Figure 9 **RSC organogram, 2007**

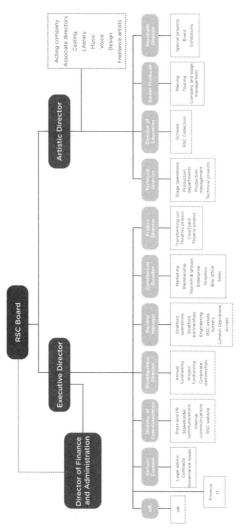

Figure 10 **RSC organisational diagram, 2008**

connected to distinct functions within the organisation – the overall effect of the diagram is far less hierarchical. The leadership functions now appear at the heart of the organisation and not at the top (see figure 10).

Changes in attitudes to the leadership

Our network analysis shows that the leadership team of Boyd and Heywood is central to both formal and informal networks at the RSC, indicating that members of staff see them as being accessible and approachable. It has been noticed that Boyd has made a point of being seen as much as possible around the organisation, and being part of everyday things, noting people's birthdays, departures, and dropping in on Staff Forums.

Our interviews support the findings of the network analysis. Members of staff were aware of the efforts made to communicate the rationale for decisions, even when those decisions were unwelcome. When we asked interviewees for their assessment of how far the organisation had progressed to becoming 'ensemble' many members of staff acknowledged and valued the effort that was being made by Boyd and Heywood, often placing their mark for 'effort' higher than that of their assessment of how ensemble the organisation had become.

Many of those interviewed said they understood the aims and objectives of the organisation and that these were clearly expressed by Boyd and Heywood. According to one senior figure, this combines well with greater operational autonomy: '[The leadership is] very clear about what they want at a broad level, but also hands-off.'

Opening up the Artistic Planning process (see chapter 4) has also had several benefits:

· Involving more departments in the planning process helps to anticipate problems and allows others more time to prepare.
· A process that was previously considered Byzantine has been demystified. One member of staff described the effect

of these changes, saying that 'previously, Artistic Planning was thought to be too commercially sensitive. It was closed formally, though everyone knew informally what was going on.'

The role of Human Resources
In both the formal and informal working networks, the Human Resources Department is noticeably more central in 2009 than in 2007. The department expanded and became more involved in different aspects of the organisation. There were three highly significant developments:

- Human Resources and Communications took responsibility for the delivery of the change process as part of a wider management team who became responsible for developing ensemble practices within their departments.
- Human Resources and Communications worked with a wide group to write and deliver the first ever staff survey in 2009.
- The devolution of employment decisions now means that managers are more willing to handle issues themselves, rather than directing members of staff to Human Resources.

In the past, the RSC had proved hostile to standard human resources techniques such as centrally held contracts and uniform procedures because they seemed to come from an alien, and non-theatrical world. Heywood comments: 'Now it is possible for Human Resources to do a lot of things such as introduce appraisals and not be feared and loathed.' [38]

As demonstration of this, when the temporary closure of the RST and Swan theatres in 2006 necessitated a second round of redundancies, the process was handled with considerably more sensitivity than the first. The first round of redundancies was guided by external consultancies and announced at a 'full company' meeting, whereas those in 2006 were managed internally and at a departmental level with full consultation taking place.

Changes in organisational resilience

Interviewees across different levels of the organisation indicated that they now feel more independent and empowered, and simultaneously better connected. One senior member of staff felt 'a lot of autonomy'. Others, from a less senior and very different part of the organisation, felt that departments that had previously felt distanced now felt as if they were 'back in the fold'. Similarly, one manager at middle-level reported that members of his team now felt 'part of a bigger picture'. Members of staff feel freer to ask questions than in the past – they also feel that communication is two-way: 'There's a feeling that you can speak up... there's more willingness to listen.'

The effect of changes in management structure
The Steering Group and Steering Committee The expansion of the Steering Group and Steering Committee (see chapter 3) had a number of advantages:

- It led to greater confidence and transparency as people felt that their opinions were being listened to and taken into account. This was especially important for those working in areas away from the administrative centre at Chapel Lane.
- It provided a forum in which change could be initiated and a clear group which could be tasked with leading it.
- At Steering Group level, in particular, transparency is valued and has helped members of middle management take greater initiative in discussing organisational decisions. As one member of the group said:

I feel personally able to say 'I fundamentally disagree with this'. [Steering Group plays] an important role of bringing different members of the company together.

Overall, changes at Steering Group level helped members develop fuller understanding of the roles of different departments within the company.

Meeting structures The change process has demanded that more time be devoted to meetings. Without such meetings and workshops things like better communication and discussion cannot happen. But now, the RSC is addressing the problem of 'too many meetings'. After discussion at Steering Group, practical steps were taken: several managers organised themselves into a cross-departmental taskforce, itself subject to a 'three meeting rule, which decided upon and framed recommendations, reporting back to Steering Group with a minimum of bureaucracy. One manager reflected:

There is still a big meeting culture here, but there is a much lighter touch now – people are questioning the purpose of meetings so that they're more useful than they used to be.

The effects of cross-departmental working

Cross-departmental working and learning has become a recognised way of meeting the different challenges faced by the RSC. It has become associated with an ensemble way of working, and is a means by which people recognise that they are working together as part of a wider whole. Staff appraisals now ask how much cross-departmental working has been undertaken, how much shadowing done and how much training of others.

Cross-departmental working has also become a way of identifying and responding to new opportunities. A good example is the RSC 'Light-Lock'. Vince Herbert, the Head of Lighting, developed a lightweight system for stabilising lights. The Legal, Marketing, Commercial, Press, Graphics and Finance departments all contributed to bringing the project to fruition. Sir Patrick Stewart from the acting company helped to produce a video to demonstrate the system and market it at a trade fair in 2008. The patented design has won two major awards. It is now going into production, and may well contribute significantly to the RSC's future income.

Evidence of cultural change
Dealing with resistance from an established organisational culture

Any process of change comes up against both anticipated and unexpected obstacles, because established ways of doing things are challenged. Ensemble was rooted in the RSC's historic traditions but it nevertheless involved reconfigurations that appeared, to some, to run against the grain of the former organisational culture.

In some departments, long-standing members of staff were brought into unfamiliar line-management relationships, and different groups that had previously been separate were brought together in the same department. For some members of staff, this was an unsettling process.

Efforts to flatten hierarchies within the organisation revealed deficiencies in management skills. People who were very good at performing their specific roles, and had achieved seniority as a result, were asked to perform additional managerial roles. It has become apparent that increasing skills and capabilities to meet new responsibilities is an essential part of managing change.

The differing views expressed at the facilitated meetings made Boyd and Heywood recognise that change was progressing at different rates in different departments. They concluded that the pace of change should not be forced and, as a result, a large-scale and organisation-wide workshop examining the collective process by which a production comes about, which had been planned for summer 2009, was postponed awaiting a departmental restructure. Boyd explained in an interview for this research: 'You cannot have an agenda in the big workshop, you need to do it honestly and be free to move forward innocently.'[39]

The postponed production workshop went ahead in January 2010. It was facilitated by Boyd, attended by 190 staff, and, for the first time, brought together all phases of the production process. The evident success of this exercise is an indication of the confidence of the organisation and Boyd's approach to personally communicating the change process.

Estimations of the extent of ensemble

On 4 May 2007, we observed a Steering Group meeting at which the penetration of the ensemble ideal was discussed. At one point Steering Group members were invited to indicate, by placing a personal sticker on a scale of 1 to 10, their response to the questions:

· Where is the RSC in terms of living the ensemble culture?
· Where am I in terms of living the ensemble culture?

Figure 11 'Where is the RSC in terms of living the ensemble culture?', 2007

Figure 12 'Where am I in terms of living the ensemble culture?', 2007

Quality and Equality Ltd 4/5/2007

Approximately half of the Steering Group attended this session, and so, like our interviews and questionnaires, it must be treated as a sample, although a representative one.

In summer 2009, we asked our interviewees the first question again in order to provide a comparison with the 2007 estimate. Responses are illustrated in Figure 13.

Figure 13 'Where is the RSC in terms of living the ensemble culture?', 2009

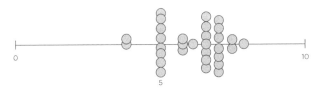

The 2007 and 2009 assessments both represent cross-sections of the organisation. It is also important to note that, by the time they were asked in 2009, interviewees had developed a more nuanced understanding of the term 'ensemble', and were also likely to have brought their own experiences of the change process to bear on their judgement. The diagrams show that:

- comparatively, judgements of progress were more positive in 2009 than 2007
- there is a similar clustering of judgements between about 5 and 7.5

We believe that by 2009 interviewees had a much clearer idea of the meaning of ensemble and, therefore, felt they had over-estimated the extent of ensemble in 2007.

In 2009, when asked for their judgement of how ensemble the organisation was, interviewees provided more elucidation of progress. In their view, the commitment to deliver ensemble should be commended, even when its achievement was incomplete. 'A 'perfect ten' was thought impossible to achieve because ensemble is considered something that is continually worked towards. Many interviewees noted a strong improvement on 2007, while commenting that any one individual's experience of ensemble would be very different. Similarly, it was thought that different departments had responded differently to the idea of ensemble.

Greater transparency and the discussion of values

In interview, a senior member of staff on the administrative side of the RSC reflected that the Staff Meetings, in which everybody meets with both Boyd and Heywood, are genuinely and, from the interviewee's experience elsewhere, almost uniquely, open. This has had several effects:

- Values have been discussed, explored and shaped as an organisation.
- Although not everyone is comfortable discussing values, doing so more freely and opening decision-making processes to

Steering Group, and sometimes beyond, has created what a senior member of staff described as:

A dynamic virtuous circle of listening, encouraging, talking. Encouraging listening leads to more trust, hence more openness hence greater efficiency and less time wasted.

- People have become more aware of what the functions of different departments are and how they come together as part of a wider whole. This affects how people feel they are valued.
- Staff also recognise that transparency around values needs careful management. Listening and discussion are seen to have their place, but the realities of any organisation, and the theatre in particular, mean that plans have to change at the last moment, which risks the process of inclusion being thought fraudulent. Boyd recognised this and opened it to discussion in the Steering Group of July 2008.

Conviviality

The efforts that the RSC has made to create opportunities for conviviality have generally been successful. Members of staff, particularly on the administrative side, appreciate the opportunities that they provide to meet others and find out about them. Despite some initial reservations the informal gathering known as Cake Friday is valued:

When I first heard that idea, I thought 'What?' [But] I think it's been fantastic – you build a better relationship with other departments.

On the other hand, Cake Friday has gone against the cultural grain of some parts of the organisation and has been counterproductive. Some departments cannot attend Cake Friday because of their commitments. 'I hate it', said one manager:

It's divisive... The rest of the organisation downs tools and [my department] can't do that... They're all eating bloody cake and drinking tea and we're here till eight o'clock.

Taking collaboration and the ensemble principle to partners: a case study

The RSC's programme for schools, the Learning and Performance Network, built on the tenets of its manifesto Stand Up for Shakespeare, is a valuable demonstration that the RSC's improved internal collaboration and changed culture also extends to the wider world. The programme currently incorporates over 300 schools. In 2009 the Centre for Education Development Appraisal and Research (CEDAR) at the University of Warwick, wrote an evaluation of the programme. It concluded that:

[The RSC's Learning and Performance Network] offers an important model of how a third sector organisation can work with higher education institutions and clusters of schools in partnership on key areas of school improvement.[40]

In particular, the ensemble nature of the hub and cluster structure that was developed was singled out and praised as encouraging 'dialogue and the building of communities of practice'. Furthermore:

One hundred per cent of lead teachers and 92 per cent of cluster schools agreed or strongly agreed that working in clusters was an effective way of improving the quality of teaching and learning across schools in a local area.[41]

The model of RSC practitioners working as 'coaches' in the local cluster schools and the ensemble model of working was observed to have 'effectively improved classroom practice and developed closer links of understanding and common purpose which will assist transition and models of progression from Year One upwards'.[42] One head teacher is quoted as saying: 'We are creating a meaningful network, not being directed to one, which I think is better.'[43]

The Stand Up for Shakespeare programme is an example of successful cultural change at the RSC. It also illustrates the exportability of the ensemble concept, and is as important a form of external validation as improved box office figures and critical success.

This belief in engagement and access extends to other areas of the RSC's work. After his appointment in 2003, Boyd initiated annual open days and free backstage tours; in 2007/08, over 10,000 people attended open days, and 5,000 attended backstage tours. Such openness is also extended to performances: before the performance of *The Grain Store* in 2009, the audience was invited to a Ukrainian feast on stage served by the actors.

5   The situation in 2010

In April 2009 the RSC commissioned Gfk NOP, a market research organisation specialising in employee research, to conduct a staff survey. In this chapter we look at the results of that survey and judge the present state of the RSC's organisational development. We also look at the way that the word ensemble has come to be overused, so that alternatives are now being developed.

Self-assessment: the 2009 staff survey

As we have shown, although the RSC at first rejected the idea of creating specific metrics to measure progress towards ensemble, it was agreed that a staff survey could be used as a benchmark to assess the organisation's progress, provided that it would be generated by the organisation and not imposed on it. Questions and process were carefully devised to work with the grain of the RSC's organisational culture. The survey set out to establish the degree of penetration of the ensemble principle in the organisation, as well as to establish staff satisfaction and the extent to which the values that the RSC leadership wished to promote were held in common.

The responses to the survey were analysed by GfK NOP, and shared with the staff at a Staff Meeting in August 2009. Overall, the survey supports many of the findings of our research, and also the leadership's judgement of progress as they described it to us. The RSC has now created its own quantitative benchmark from which to judge future progress, right across the organisation.

Overall findings

The survey revealed: that members of staff feel very high
levels of satisfaction and pride in working for the RSC;
ensemble is fully understood as a concept by three–quarters
of the organisation; there is a belief that the RSC is strongly
led, but there is a less clear understanding of management
structures. Ensemble values and the management structures
that have been put in place to support them are rated more
highly in administrative than in technical parts of the
organisation. Physical geography has a strong influence on
the penetration of the ensemble principle and the relationship
between responses and length of service confirms the cultural
differences we observed in our research.

Evidence and opinion from elsewhere provide a
context to the findings of the RSC's Staff Survey. In
November 2009, the Department for Business, Innovation
and Skills published *Engaging for Success: Enhancing
performance through employee engagement,* which points
out that 'engagement, going to the heart of the workplace
relationship between employee and employer, can be a
key to unlocking productivity'.[45] In October 2009, the
Chartered Institute of Management released figures that
show that 65 per cent of its members said morale had
worsened in the previous six months, and 42 per cent
reported a deterioration in employee engagement.[46]

Satisfaction

The RSC's survey shows very high levels of satisfaction that
are relatively consistent across the whole organisation. The
staff survey also indicates national averages for the public and
private sectors by way of comparison.

· 82 per cent of staff agreed they 'would recommend the RSC as
  a company to work for'. (The average response for the public
  sector is 55 per cent, for the private sector 64 per cent.)
· 72 per cent said they were satisfied with their job.
  (Average satisfaction in the public sector 64 per cent, private
  sector 67 per cent.)

- 80 per cent said they were satisfied with the RSC as an employer. (Average satisfaction in the public sector 65 per cent, private sector 69 per cent.)

There are also very high levels of pride in the organisation: 92 per cent agreed with the statement: 'I am proud to work with the RSC'. This compares very favourably with 61 per cent in the public sector and 67 per cent in the private sector.

Ensemble working and values

About half of the organisation agrees that it works according to ensemble principles. This concurs with both the findings of our interviews, and Boyd's own assessment: 'We are about 50 per cent of the way there'.[47]

Figure 14 illustrates the survey results relating to the RSC's three publicly stated aims of:

- working through the principles of ensemble
- engaging with the world
- connecting people with Shakespeare.

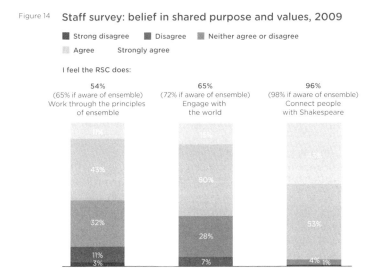

Figure 14 **Staff survey: belief in shared purpose and values, 2009**

■ Strong disagree ■ Disagree ■ Neither agree or disagree
■ Agree Strongly agree

I feel the RSC does:

54% (65% if aware of ensemble) Work through the principles of ensemble	65% (72% if aware of ensemble) Engage with the world	96% (98% if aware of ensemble) Connect people with Shakespeare
11%		
43%		5%
	56%	
	50%	
32%		53%
	28%	
11%		
3%	7%	4% 1%

When these findings are broken down by different functional groups within the organisationand combined with the data provided by the survey in relation to the RSC's core values of being 'ambitious', 'engaging', 'enquiring' and 'collaborative', the differences we had observed in our interviews between departments were confirmed. They are shown in figure 15. Figure 15 shows that:

- Technical departments are less confident than other departments that the RSC is collaborative; they are also less likely to think that the RSC works according to ensemble principles.
- Departments based in Chapel Lane – particularly the Commercial, Marketing and Executive teams – tend to agree more than other departments that the organisation works in collaborative ways and is ensemble; responses also indicated that these departments are more in agreement than others that the organisation works according to its stated values.
- A sense of the organisation's ambition is consistently high across all departments. This echoes the importance of what we have called 'pulse points', the momentum that the organisation draws from setting itself ambitious targets (see chapter 2).

The survey results also confirmed our finding that, as a concept, ensemble is understood (see figure 16), but it has yet to fully permeate the organisation in relation to practice.

When interviewed before the details of the staff survey had been analysed, Boyd anticipated this response, saying the split comes with 'the nitty-gritty of life in a department'.[48]

Influence of length of service
Length of service is revealed as a major factor in determining people's opinion. Staff who have been at the RSC for less than a year are more likely to agree that 'their opinion counts' (62 per cent) compared with 38 per cent of those who have been at the RSC for more than 20 years; of those who have been in the organisation for less than a year, 70 per cent 'feel supported by the RSC in their work' compared with 47 per cent of those

Figure 15 **Staff survey: differing attitudes to core values, 2009**

■ RSC

■ IT, HR, Finance, Executive Office, Health and Safety

■ Estates, General Counsel, Project Office

■ Development, Press and Communications, Marketing, Commercial Services

■ Acting Company

■ Artistic Director, Producers, Education, Events and Exhibitions, Voice,
Movement, Associate Directors, Casting, Literary, Music, Stage Management,
Company Management

■ Technical –Workshops, Hire Wardrobe

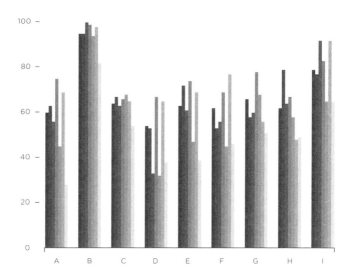

A = I am familiar with the 3 elements of the RSC's purpose

B = I feel the RSC does connect people with Shakespeare

C = I feel the RSC does engage with the world

D = I feel the RSC does work through the principles of ensemble

E = I am familiar with the 4 values

F = I feel the RSC is collaborative — works together

G = I feel the RSC is inquiring — finds new ways of doing things

H = I feel the RSC is engaging — puts audiences at the heart of the work

I = I feel the RSC is ambitious — committed to excellence

Figure 16 **Staff survey: attitudes to ensemble, 2009**

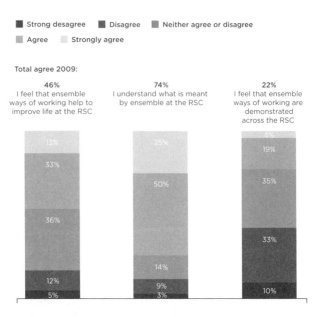

■ Strong desagree   ■ Disagree   ■ Neither agree or disagree
■ Agree   ■ Strongly agree

Total agree 2009:

46%	74%	22%
I feel that ensemble ways of working help to improve life at the RSC	I understand what is meant by ensemble at the RSC	I feel that ensemble ways of working are demonstrated across the RSC

who have been there for more than 20 years. As with our
interviews, this reveals different expectations of the workplace
within the RSC. Similarly, the survey concluded that 'support
for ensemble ways of working is highest amongst the new and
recent joiners', with 69 per cent of those who have been at the
RSC for up to two years feeling that 'ensemble improves life at
the RSC', compared with 39 per cent of those who have been
there between five and 20 years.

Management
Although the survey results in relation to management are
less positive than those showing levels of satisfaction, they
are still higher at the RSC than the averages in the public and
private sectors. When asked whether managers 'provide a clear
sense of direction for the company', 58 per cent of staff agreed
(public sector average 36 per cent, private sector 51 per cent).

Geography influences perceptions of management. Boyd, Heywood and senior management have offices at Chapel Lane, in Stratford-upon-Avon, and Earlham Street in London. Staff at both these locations are the most likely to say that they are 'talked to by senior management about issues affecting the company'; the least likely to agree with this statement are those based at Arden Street and Timothy's Bridge Road.

What does the staff survey tell us?

The staff survey and the research undertaken for this report demonstrate that considerable progress has been made by the RSC in the last three years. Embedding cultural change is normally at least a five-year endeavour, so the RSC's achievement has been relatively rapid. It is, of course, unfinished, as the organisation and its leaders recognise. The RSC has been attempting to change the organisation at two levels simultaneously: working within each area or department, and working across areas and departments. Organisational gain is likely to be greatest in the latter case, and it is here that the RSC appears to have had greatest success.

Any attempt at organisational change is likely to meet some resistance in exactly the places where the RSC has found resistance: in specialised functions that concentrate on a narrow area where there is little need to collaborate extra-departmentally in order to meet the task in hand, and where collaboration and consultation can thus be seen as time-wasting; and in some members of staff who have grown used to one way of working and feel uncomfortable with change. What is surprising at the RSC is both the relatively low level of resistance, and the relatively rapid speed with which change has been adopted. The reasons why this is the case are discussed in chapter 7.

Fatigue with the word 'ensemble' – but not with the concept

Some RSC staff members think that ensemble means better consultation, teamwork, openness and a feeling of being part of a shared endeavour. For others, the word implies a much more egalitarian process, with everyone having an equal say in decision making. It is widely recognised that the latter is impossible, but this can debase the rhetoric, and a degree of cynicism starts to creep in.

While the word 'ensemble' has proved valuable in providing a familiar, artistic term for many of the principles associated with organisational change, it has also proved problematic. Some interviewees for this research rejected the word, because of its foreignness and ambiguity, while respecting the values it represents. Boyd himself explained the problem:

The term 'ensemble' has currency with the actors and a lot of currency with ordinary desk-jobs; it has worse than no currency with areas in which it feels like a fucking French word used by some English liberal.[49]

As the change process has developed and more members of staff have become familiar with the term and the values that it represents, the valency of ensemble has also changed within the RSC. At the time of our interviews in 2007, Boyd and Heywood's vision of extending ensemble to the organisation as a whole was recognised by some, but the term 'ensemble' was more generally thought of as either 'a flash word put into a mission statement' or as something based entirely in the rehearsal room. By the time of our second analysis, it was widely recognised as a useful organisational principle that acted as shorthand for the way that the organisation was developing. However, it had also become used both as a tongue-in-cheek means of calling people to account, and as a means of satirising the process, for example, taking the last chocolate biscuit at Cake Friday can be condemned as being 'not very ensemble'.

Senior management has therefore started to move away from using the word 'ensemble' to describe the process of change at the RSC. One senior member of staff confirmed this:

I would try not to use that word ensemble, I think it had its moment in helping us to define something but I also think that it means something very specific in different forms of theatre and so I rather think of it and describe it as the doing, which is working together.

As Heywood puts it:

We started to realise that it was beginning to lose currency because it was being over-used... We held back from a big push on communications until we had some actual things to be talking about rather than just a 'way of being', which... starts to get quite fluffy, even a gag. So when that started to happen we decided to concentrate on demonstrating the sort of behaviours that we wanted to see, if you are in the RSC.[50]

6   Future questions

In this chapter we present a set of questions that the RSC now faces in relation to ensemble, some of which would be faced by any organisation at a similar stage of development.

In her early work as change-facilitator with the RSC's senior management, Dr Cheung-Judge used a five-phase model of organisational cultural change to describe the stages through which an organisation reinvents itself:

1 *Deformative phase*: a period, often of crisis, that provides the stimulus for change.

2 *Reconciliative phase*: a fresh start is made where people come together to tackle the problem and renew the organisation's vision.

3 *Acculturative phase*: the vision begins to become a reality as the whole organisation is aligned to a common purpose and a common culture is established.

4 *Enactive phase*: management structures and working practices are changed. Cultural meanings become cultural practice in everyday behaviour.

5 *Formative phase*: the 'new' culture is established and achieves structural form.

In our judgement, the RSC is now reaching the end of the enactive phase, and a number of formal structures are in place to ensure that the cultural change that has been achieved will be sustained. But organisations never stand still. The RSC is committed to being a 'learning organisation' and therefore in a state of continuous development. The external environment also changes and, when one issue is settled, it often stimulates a new set of questions.

Leaving aside consideration of the external environment affecting box office takings, fundraising and publicly supported theatre in a recession, there are challenges ahead in the form of further organisational reform and development.

Principally, the RSC faces the task of developing a more sophisticated understanding of the idea of ensemble beyond the senior and middle management level of Steering Group. The results of the staff survey suggest that, while the values of ensemble are widely understood, only about half of respondents thought that they are reflected in day-to-day practice throughout the organisation. As Boyd recognises: 'At some point, we have to trust the [Steering] Group and share it beyond into the organisation. It cannot just be me and Vikki speaking three times a year.' [51]

'Sharing it' will place new demands on middle managers and staff, who will need to develop new skills, while the organisation as a whole will need to continue to respect craft and technical skills. 'Sharing it' will also make demands on people's time, when they would rather be 'getting on with the job'. Paradoxically, closer contact between staff uncovers differences between them, whereas the principle of ensemble is intended to diminish senses of difference and hierarchy.

Specific tasks that remain include:

· Clarifying the respective roles of Steering Group, Steering Committee and Artistic Planning to make it more obvious where and when decision making occurs.
· Continuing to strengthen the links between different geographic locations in order to lessen differences caused by other factors such as different working hours, different functions and different terms of service.
· Getting the pace of change right: keeping up momentum while avoiding consulting and discussing too much.
· Deciding how far into the organisation the ensemble principle should reach. There are specialist roles that can

be accomplished without much contact with the rest of the organisation, so how important is it that everyone feels part of the wide ensemble?

· Considering how far to extend the ensemble principle to ensure that the audience and public are part of the ensemble.

The RSC has a long-term ambition to re-establish a London presence, but would require access to a thrust stage similar to that of the new RST and Swan theatres. No such stage at present exists. This technical matter raises a number of important issues, including the sustainability of a London presence, and the effect on the organisation of running two large theatres 100 miles apart. The two thrust stages in Stratford will become the physical embodiment of an ensemble of actors, audience, technicians and front of house. The lack of a similar space in London will inevitably begin to push the organisation to resolve the 'London problem' by providing a similar experience.

There are three further questions:

· Can the RSC successfully reconcile the principle of ensemble acting with the box office pressure to have star names on the bill?

· Is it ever possible wholly to resolve the 'ensemble paradox': that in the end, on the stage and in the boardroom, someone has to take the final decision, and that the collectivism of ensemble nonetheless needs strong leadership?

· Organisational change at the RSC has been driven by a strong leadership team. What happens when new leaders take over? Can, and should, the working practices of ensemble be sacrosanct and unchangeable for a new set of leaders?

7   Lessons learned

In this chapter we suggest what other organisations might learn from the RSC's experience. These are grouped under three headings: leadership, networks, and creativity and change.

Organisational change is a non-linear process, affected by pre-existing organisational culture, the relationships between individuals, and specific external circumstances, all of which applied in the case of the RSC.

It is for these reasons that we have titled this chapter 'Lessons learned' rather than calling it a 'toolkit'. We firmly believe that the RSC's experience offers valuable lessons that have a more general application, but we caution against the idea that replicating language, structures or practices from one organisation into another inevitably generates predictable results.

Leadership

As we have seen in chapter 2, it is a paradox of ensemble that the organic development of a co-operative and empowered organisational culture nevertheless depends on the direction and coherence provided by leadership. The RSC's progress over the course of our research clearly demonstrates the need for effective leadership. What we mean by 'effective leadership' is the ability to marry rhetorical power with practical innovations so as to create a sustainable, resilient, well-networked organisation, capable of growing its own capacity to act, and providing high-quality results for its customers, staff and funders.

Leadership should be shared and distributed

The RSC's story shows that it is not the titles and conventions of leadership that matter, but what leaders do and how they do it. Much of the rhetoric around leadership concentrates on the individual – 'the right person at the top' – but research shows that companies, in the creative sector at least, may have a single individual as the public face, but have strong teams acting as collective leaders.[52] At the RSC – and in theatre and the arts more widely – the model of explicit shared leadership between artistic and managerial roles is far from novel: the National Theatre, for instance, has both an (Artistic) Director and an Executive Director. Other sectors should learn to think of leadership as embedded within a wider group, and as a flexible activity that can be successfully shared in many ways. The generally accepted term for this in leadership theory is 'distributed leadership'.[53]

Leaders need to use the right language and metaphors

It has been important to find some word or term that both acts as a metaphor for distributed leadership and fits organisational culture. At the RSC it has been the term 'ensemble'. Other organisations will need to find a phrase that fits their own culture and sector, but everyone needs a shorthand that sends the same set of messages: that people will have a voice, take responsibility for both themselves and others, and work to a common end. Whatever term is chosen, it needs to be adaptable to the way that the organisation develops, and leaders must be alive to when the language needs to change.

Leaders need to embody the values that they promote

Strong and distinctive organisational cultures, resting on explicit values, have been recognised as key factors in successful organisations.[54]

References to values are a constant feature in the RSC's ensemble journey. Boyd has repeatedly emphasised the need for honesty, altruism, tolerance, forgiveness, humility and magnanimity. One of the main tasks of leaders is to articulate and reiterate organisational values and link them, in one direction, to the individual and, in the other, to the wider world.

Any disparity between the rhetoric of values and what happens on the ground damages organisations (as Google found out when the gap between its corporate slogan 'Don't be evil' and its dealings with the Chinese government created a storm of protest).[55] Equally, values need to connect inwardly so that they are apparent in everyday practices and the quality of relationships. When the values expressed are disconnected from the norms of behaviour within an organisation it leads to cynicism, and poor morale and performance.

But leaders cannot simply communicate values – they have to do more. In an organisational context, discussion of values can often seem artificial and remote from everyday life. Lofty pronouncements from the board or CEO seem divorced from the pressures of getting things done. Leaders have to provide the spaces and places, and the time, for values to be explored, discussed, disputed, agreed and internalised. They also have to 'walk the talk' and be personally responsible for living up to the organisation's values.

Sustainable organisational change can only come about if the rhetoric of the way the organisation operates is matched by the quality of relationships that it produces.

Leaders need to lead the change process

Organisational change, wherever it is attempted, takes place in a context where the organisation is busy and short of time, where external factors demand attention, and where there will be some internal resistance. Organisational development is easily set back by such obstacles, but all of them should be expected and anticipated by leaders who want to foster change, even though the particular forms taken will be unpredictable. Leaders need not only to demonstrate confidence in the change process but also to be deeply involved in the minutiae of change: sustainable change can only come from within, it cannot be imposed from without. Leaders must also be committed to leading the change process: they can use external help and support, but change cannot be sub-contracted or outsourced.

Leaders must acknowledge emotions

A remarkable feature of the RSC's leadership and management style has been the regular and explicit reference to emotions.

In his speech at the New York Public Library in June 2008, Michael Boyd used words like terror, daring, fear, empathy, compassion and love, 'which I say without any apology'. Indeed he uses the word 'love' ten times.[56] Very few leaders in government or the corporate sector speak so openly about the emotions that everyone knows are a major feature of organisational life. There are exceptions. In the Institute of Directors' magazine, *Director,* of June 2009, Tim Smit of the Eden Project was described as 'an inspirational leader' partly because 'he marries vision and emotion with pragmatism'. But acknowledging emotions is seen as odd and mysterious – the magazine article is titled 'Casting a spell'.[57]

Leaders often avoid talking about the emotional life of an organisation – it is seen as odd, embarrassing, and soft. But emotions exist, and when harnessed in the right way, are a powerful force. As Linda Holbeche, an expert in organisational change, says:

Managing change effectively requires more than an intellectual understanding of the processes involved. It requires... real emotional, political and some would say spiritual intelligence on the part of those leading change.[58]

Leaders should provide conceptual simplicity in response to organisational and contextual complexity

Every large-scale organisation is complex, and every organisation exists within a changing and multifaceted context. Difficult and demanding tasks need to be underpinned by clear and comprehensible concepts that everyone understands and can feel part of intellectually and emotionally. A good example of an organisation that got this right is NASA. When President Kennedy visited the NASA Space Centre, he asked a cleaner what his job was, and the cleaner replied: 'Putting a man on the moon'. The RSC offers a more modest, but equally compelling case of a complex organisation with a simple message. When asked what was the purpose of the RSC, our interviewees repeatedly expressed the same aspiration: to be the best theatre for Shakespeare in the world.

Leaders are at the heart of a network, not at the top of a pyramid
As Henry Mintzberg puts it:

A robust community requires a form of leadership quite different from the models that have it driving transformation from the top. Community leaders see themselves as being in the centre, reaching out rather than down.[59]

In chapter 4, we show how the RSC moved from visualising the organisation as a hierarchy to seeing it more like a mind-map, see figure 10, with leadership placed as a central resource. Creating strong networks is one of the most vital tasks of contemporary leadership.

Networks
It is important to create and strengthen networks within organisations
There are numerous examples of how new and strengthened networks have helped the RSC to operate to better effect. Networks are important because:

- They encourage innovation: networks create links that allow things to happen – for example the commercial exploitation of a new lighting invention at the RSC became possible because of the newly forged relationships between half a dozen departments, see chapter 4.
- They promote efficiency: networks produce collective, effective and speedy decisions – for example the changes in artistic forward planning detailed in chapter 3.
- They make organisations resilient: networks enable self-organisation and generate the capacity to respond to events in the right way.
- They promote individual welfare: networks allow individuals to flourish within a collective, because they provide support, and connection to a greater whole.

Networks need a common language of words, metaphors and symbols

The words that leaders use have to resonate and have meaning across a whole organisation. A common language helps networks to form and eases communication. Ensemble is a founding concept at the RSC, and the word itself appeals both to tradition and to the specialism of a particular discipline – the theatre. It thus helps to create unity. The word 'group' or 'team' could have been used instead of ensemble but neither would have had the same resonance or the same sense of history.

Networks grow organically, and it can also be helpful to use words, like ensemble, that are ambiguous, because that allows for development, creativity and exploration.

Within networks, seemingly small acts and moments can gain extraordinary potency – both positive and negative. Leaders need to have heightened sensitivity to the way that meaning gathers around symbols and metaphors and the way that people project big ideas onto the detail of their lives. For example, in addition to changing the way that networks operate through interaction in physical space, the new RST building will be a powerful symbol of a renewed RSC. In a sense, it will be a multi-million pound metaphor for the way that the organisation has changed not only itself, but also its relationships with the outside world – from its audiences to its locality and to its supporters.

Networks are strengthened through learning and self-reflection

The RSC has created many formal and informal opportunities for people to learn not just about things that are immediately relevant to their jobs, but much more widely, see chapter 3. Our conclusion is that learning is valuable not only for the individual, but also because it increases the number and quality of interactions in an organisation, leading to more conviviality, better communication and improved mutual understanding.

One feature of the RSC's development over the last seven years has been continuous self-reflection. At various points on the path to changing the organisation, leaders and larger groups of staff have taken stock of where they have come from, where they are and where they are going. The techniques used to undertake self-reflection have ranged from a consciously structured whole-company staff survey, through managerial or departmental gatherings, to one-to-one meetings.

Self-awareness within a network creates constant sources of feedback, which mean that corrective or beneficial action takes place more speedily, and can take the form of 'nudges' and 'tweaks' rather than sudden and violent changes of direction. An example is the way in which the use of the word ensemble is itself being slowly dropped from written communications and in discussions because it has started to become overused.

Networks need to be open and transparent

The RSC has moved from being a hierarchical organisation steeped in secrecy, where information was closely guarded and decisions taken by individuals or small groups, to one that is much more open. This has been particularly the case in the Human Resources, Finance and Artistic Planning departments. The beneficial effects of these changes and the resultant gains in efficiency are detailed in chapter 4, but it should be noted that these gains have been made possible by the relatively free flow of data and information around the networked organisation. The more information moves around a network, the more the network itself is strengthened.

Networks help overcome 'silos'

Studies attest to the fact that people work better and are happier in their work when they have a large degree of autonomy and control over what they do.[60] The experience of many companies confirms that flattening hierarchies, giving people more responsibility, and encouraging questioning, improves performance.

However, the simple devolution of power risks creating silos and a series of units at war with each other. It can also lead to inefficiencies when disparate ways of doing things fail to mesh with each other. The desired state is therefore one where autonomy, individual responsibility and collective responsibility all increase.

Combining individual action with systemic consistency across a networked organisation (as opposed to directing action through a hierarchy) depends on people trusting each other. As Paul Skidmore puts it in *Network Logic:*

Leaders carry responsibility to preserve the trust on which their networks depend. In an unpredictable world in which some failures are almost bound to happen, that is a tough challenge. Acknowledging our interdependence with others, and the limited capacity of our leaders to manage it, will be a frightening experience. It is much more convenient to think that leaders will be saviours – and that we have someone to blame when things do not go our way. But if it wakes us up to the potential within each of us to solve our own problems, then so much the better.[61]

At the RSC, it is recognised that leaders cannot have all the answers, but there is a strong belief in the leaders' sincerity, and that they will always try to do the right thing. As one member of the team put it:

They [Boyd, Heywood and other senior managers], the powers that be, are trying to make it a positive and uplifting experience for everyone and I think that it is working.

Sensitivity to individual perspectives and recognising that everyone's contribution increases a sense of belonging

The RSC has found a number of ways to accommodate the needs of individuals and has acted to make sure that those needs are met. One example is consideration of different standpoints on organisational decisions. As one interviewee put it: 'You actually do matter... There is a genuine effort to make each person a valued member of staff.'

In addition, efforts are made to recognise everyone's contribution to the organisation. For example, the RSC lists all staff alphabetically within their departments in its performance programmes (as reproduced at the end of this report). This seemingly small idea is emblematic of something that is in fact very important. It demonstrates the RSC's ecological sensibility – that is, it shows an understanding that every part is needed to make a whole, and that every element is as vital as every other in creating a complete system. This is recognised in management theory:

In a context that is fast-moving, complicated and unpredictable, the notion of organisations as living, complex, adaptive systems seems particularly apt.[62]

It is also recognised in other successful companies, such as Pixar, where:

The technical people and the artists are peers with each other. We do not have one in a second class to the other, we don't think that one is more important than the other; rather they're all coming together for the purpose of the story.[63]

Networks are powerfully affected by buildings and design

As described in chapter 3, during the period of our research, different parts of the RSC have moved premises, and people were doing their jobs in different spaces and places, be that offices or theatres.

The experience of the RSC shows that physical remoteness is difficult to overcome, and that it is easier to form working relationships when everyone is together in the same place. What is equally clear is that buildings and spaces have affects as well as effects. In other words, places have their own psycho-geography, and the quality of the relationships within a network is affected by the way that physical spaces encourage or inhibit contact and communications. The thrust stage at the RST clearly demonstrates this understanding, as it is intended to transform the relationship between actor and audience.

Creativity and change

Organisational change is not easy. According to Linda Holbeche: 'Various reports suggest that 75 per cent of all transformation efforts fail.'[64] Leaders have to hold in balance on the one hand an organisation's creativity and desire to change, and on the other its continuity, established culture and traditions.[65] The experience of the RSC shows some ways in which this can be done.

Crisis can provide an opportunity for change, but ambition and energy are what make change happen

President Obama's Chief of Staff, Rahm Emanuel, is credited with saying: 'You never let a serious crisis go to waste. They are opportunities to do big things.'[66] Bill George, Management Professor at Harvard, says the same thing: 'Never waste a good crisis.'[67] The RSC's experience bears witness to the fact that people are more willing to accept radical change in times of crisis.

But once the need for change is recognised, the next step is to create a sense of coherence, so that effort can be directed to a shared set of priorities rather than dissipated in a flurry of fire-fighting responses. The RSC's experience shows that big, ambitious priorities concentrate effort and energy.

Over the last five years the RSC has set itself a number of tasks that have stretched every fibre of the company, including the staging of The Complete Works Festival, The Histories, Stand up for Shakespeare, and the remodelling of the RST, Chapel Lane and other parts of the organisation's Stratford-upon-Avon estate. It is the scale of the ambition and the clarity of the goals that have provided the context in which many different detailed tasks have come together to produce the desired results. A big, shared ambition encourages collaboration. It helps generate responsibility and encourages communication and efficiency because people realise that the goal can only be achieved by working together.

The experience of the RSC shows that energy is needed to push organisational development forward. That energy can be injected by leaders (such as when Boyd and Heywood address meetings); it can come from external sources (such as outside facilitators); and it can come from creating 'pulse points' where the whole organisation is stretched to achieve a specific goal.

Experimentation and constant small-scale innovations help change to happen

There are many advantages in undertaking organisational innovation on a limited but continuous experimental basis because such an approach:

- is less threatening than major change
- can be retracted if the innovation proves problematic
- is easier to slow down or speed up than large-scale change
- is less expensive than wholesale change
- creates momentum and stimulus
- focuses energy
- develops confidence
- provides opportunities for celebration
- acknowledges that different parts of an organisation move at a different pace

A good way to experiment with change is through inter-disciplinary, task-oriented, time-limited teamwork. The RSC set about addressing a number of issues, such as the feeling that there were too many meetings, by setting up teams of people from across a range of departments to come up with suggestions for reform. These endeavours were not always 100 per cent successful, and some people thought that too much time was spent on meetings and discussion through this process. Nevertheless, our view is that setting up teams of people who bring different experience and perspectives to a specific task which they have to achieve within a particular time (in this case in no more than three meetings) is a good approach. It works best where expectations of the process and the potential outcomes are set in advance, and where there is a level of commitment to implement the suggested changes so that people don't feel they are wasting their time and effort.

Changing things depends on creating confidence and trust
Leaders need to develop the confidence of their staff that what
they are doing is right and will work. The RSC did this partly
by seeking outside advice and validation to affirm what they
were doing, but they then understood that they needed to 'ride
their own bicycle'. Implementing change is also helped when
there is trust in leadership – not necessarily trust that leaders
will always get it right, but trust that they will try to do the
right thing, and always act in what they believe to be the best
interests of the organisation and the people within it. Creating
and maintaining trust is a tough challenge, but is also one of
the most important tasks of contemporary leadership.

Change needs to be tested internally and externally
One danger of change processes within organisations, with
their accompanying concentration on internal focus and more
frequent discussion groups, is that they can lose touch with
external realities. Inspiring rhetoric and charismatic leadership
on their own are not enough. Once a company believes its own
propaganda it is in dangerous territory, as the case of Enron
clearly shows. The RSC benefits from being unable to insulate
itself from outside judgement – every play goes in front of the
critics – but it has also sought to test its own understandings
by the frequent involvement of outsiders. Indeed, the commissioning of this report has provided one such external check.

The realisation of creativity rests on collaboration
As a successful cultural organisation, the RSC lives and
breathes artistic creativity. But every organisation has to
adapt, innovate and be creative to some degree. The RSC's
experience shows that creativity can only be realised through
collective and collaborative endeavour, and the more that is
facilitated – through good communications, a strong common
culture, the creation of the right set of attitudes, and so
on – the more likely it is that the organisation will be able to
experiment, and hence to innovate well, across its whole range
of activities.

Epilogue: the Hamlet crisis

Just before the RSC's *Hamlet* transferred from Stratford-upon-Avon to London in late 2008, the actor playing Hamlet, David Tennant, was injured, and was unable to play the lead at very late notice on the day of the key press night. The choice the RSC faced was either to pull the performance or to keep faith with the ensemble, its commitment to the understudy rehearsal training process, and the strength of the whole company of actors.

In a press release of 8 December 2008, Boyd and the RSC made a public statement:

As an ensemble company we feel that it is important to go ahead with tonight's performance. While understanding that some people will be disappointed at not seeing David Tennant on stage, this production, like all our productions, is more than the sum of its parts – an ensemble of actors, designers, composers etc. and we should respect that by going ahead as planned.[68]

The RSC held firm to its ensemble beliefs and Ed Bennett, Tennant's understudy, took the stage to great critical acclaim. From an organisational perspective, many departments: Actors, Directors, Designers, Box Office, Web, Marketing, Communications, Human Resources, London Operations, Development, Legal, Voice, Movement, Producers, Production, Wardrobe, Stage Management, Props and Lighting, collaborated quickly and smoothly to avoid letting the audiences and company down. Ensemble provided the resilience, organisational capacity and rhetorical power to turn what could have been a defining crisis for the strength of the RSC's core identity into a resounding endorsement of the principles and values of ensemble.

Afterword

A comment from Dr Mee-Yan Cheung-Judge

Background and context

In the 1980s, there was an explosion of 'guru-led' change-management theories. These focused on metrics and measurements, technical systems and process design. In the main, they considered business process improvement or organisational structure – things like headcount, roles, skills and capacity. The promised improvements and savings from this type of expert-led approach to change often failed to materialise. Once the consultants had left, implementation usually proved far harder to achieve than was expected, and change did not 'stick'.

A 2008 survey showed that companies in the UK lost £1.7 billion a year from failed change initiatives; across Western Europe, approximately €10 billion is wasted on ineffective business process change projects each year.[69] The missing element tended to be a failure to address cultural alignment, behavioural shift and people engagement – the three key components that make change stick. This is why the case of the RSC, in which cultural change was tackled, is so interesting.

Arts organisations tend to be reluctant to engage external support for change projects. They know instinctively that 'guru-led', formula-based change methodology is not palatable to their organisational culture. Tailor-made, creative solutions that focus on mobilising people's passion and commitment suit them better.

I am a practitioner from a field called Organisational Development (OD). This discipline recognises that organisations are complex, adaptive and essentially human systems. It uses tailored processes that fit into a specific organisation's cultural context, and emphasises methodology that unleashes imagination, engagement, participation and empowerment. OD practitioners recognise that without sufficient energy from key individuals and groups within an organisation, there is little hope of change being sustained organically even if the change is strategically important. Using this type of approach to change eased my entrance to the RSC. Within a short time of being asked to help, the RSC and I were able to agree on how to approach the ensemble change initiative.

So, the first insight is that there are methodologies that are a better fit for the cultural sector. These methodologies, once understood, can also be easily picked up by the leaders of an organisation to apply to their organisational change without undue dependence on external people, as in the case of the RSC.

Applying Organisational Development to the RSC
Three principles underlie the OD approach to change:

· identifying the correct type of change and focusing on the 'end game'
· securing the engagement of key people
· using 'high leverage' change methodology

I describe them below showing how we put them into practice at the RSC.

Identifying the correct type of change and focusing on the 'end game'
The ensemble-change at the RSC is an internally initiated change with the intention of spreading what works from the theatre to the rest of the organisation. The objective is to bed down the ensemble culture in people's day-to-day behaviour. The change is hence primarily a cultural alignment and a behavioural exercise, but with a clear strategic intention.

In OD methodology, once the nature of change has been worked out, the next job is to focus on the 'end game'. At the RSC, the end game was to align individual paradigms and behaviour with the organisation's ensemble culture. This required at least three levels of system intervention: *the individual level*, *the group (inter-group) level* and the level of the *total organisation*. This entailed:

- providing specific, individual experiences (mainly through dialogue) so that people can examine their own paradigm and modify behaviour themselves
- creating a 'cultural island' experience for groups so that in those change interventions, old norms can be challenged and new norms can be experimented with, without risk
- aligning the organisation's systems and processes to reinforce and support the change paradigm and behaviour.

At the RSC, we involved people in identifying the collective desired outcomes of change. This gave people the opportunity to contribute to creating the conditions by which the RSC could achieve those outcomes. We designed interventions to connect people to each other so that those who understood the ensemble concept instinctively could influence the more apprehensive. Finally, the Human Resources and Communication departments carried out a number of initiatives to bed change down in the RSC's organisational systems and processes.

Securing the engagement of key people

Successful change depends on identifying and securing the engagement of key individuals and groups. I worked with Vikki Heywood and Michael Boyd to identify:

- the key individuals and groups on whom change would depend
- those who held data that we, as the change team, did not have
- those whose perspectives were needed to provide a more robust way of thinking about change

We paid a lot of attention to human dynamics because the RSC is full of political complexity and staffed with individuals who have high aspirations for the organisation and their art. We knew most people in the RSC would like to take part in determining the change processes. The principle that governed our thinking was that 'people will support what they help to create'.[70]

Our first step was to engage the Steering Committee, the Steering Group and middle management before making the change agenda public within the rest of the organisation. Without endorsement at this level, the project would have been vulnerable, so an intervention was designed to help people to personalise the reasons why taking an ensemble approach to change might be good, and to encourage people to discuss their doubts and hesitations openly. My job was to support Heywood and Boyd in considering what type of processes would help to acknowledge and work with any conflict and resistance encountered in these top groups. Interventions were designed to enroll the help of these key groups in supporting the implementation of solutions with the rest of the organisation in the next phase.

Using 'high leverage' change methodology

'High leverage' methodologies 'create high energy and yield extraordinary sustainable results'.[71] Such methodologies have been proven to reduce implementation time over more directive methods by half.[72] There are a number of key elements to 'high leverage' methods.

They are dialogue based Any change that challenges people's personal 'worldview' or paradigm cannot rely on the 'tell and sell' approach: a structured dialogue and inquiry approach is much more effective. In any culture-change process, people need the freedom to have a voice, be heard, dream, be passionate, co-construct, participate and contribute. Positive psychological approaches such as 'appreciative inquiry' work best. We used this at the RSC, especially in the intervention that took the form of a staff conference, where we started the process with a pair interview: using the themes of the interview, we invited people to co-construct how change should be approached and what conditions would support it.

They are whole system based, surface-diverse perspectives

Change, particularly culture-change processes, must encourage the various parts of a system to connect with each other. People support change more if they have opportunities to share understanding of the need to change, analyse current reality, identify what needs to change, generate ideas on how to change and map out an implementation plan. It is important to engage multiple perspectives, and give different stakeholders the opportunity to influence each other. This strengthens debate and helps people find common ground. From my experience, common ground will only emerge after the diverse views held within an organisation have been properly debated. At the RSC, a number of conflicting perspectives did emerge, and Heywood and Boyd listened to those voices and adjusted the speed and content of the change programme accordingly, hence creating a safe atmosphere in which change could happen.

Emotions matters and are crucial data

All changes arouse emotions, positive as well as negative. If these are not properly managed, the change outcome will be at risk. OD recognises people's desire to shape their own destinies; if people understand why and where change is needed, they can work out the implementation and are more likely to support change than if they are simply told what will happen. All the change processes we designed at the RSC aimed to encourage people to share not just their view but also their emotions – this is especially important for a creative organisation where emotions are a core part of their creative resources. Heywood, Boyd and the change team did a great job in managing individuals' emotions. Through their commitment to the change process, they provided what I call an 'emotional anchor' for the staff.

Managing psychological transition OD focuses on the transition process rather just the outcome to which it aspires. It is not the change outcome that trips people up – it is the transition journey that does the damage.[73] OD must therefore manage people's experiences of transition, delivering change in such a way as to ensure there is a 'safe arrival'. By involving the RSC staff as early as possible, I relied on their 'native instinct' in identifying how best to manage the different concerns that emerged from the change journey.

Leverage the covert processes to deliver results Most people tend to use the rational and logical 'business cases' to mobilise people in change. However, out of the six dimensions of change, five are covert. Bob Marshak has shown that change needs to work beyond the level of reason (rationality, analysis and logic) and extend to addressing organisational *politics* (individual and group interests), *inspirations* (values-based and visionary aspirations), *emotions* (affective and reactive feelings), *mindsets* (guiding beliefs and assumptions) and *psychodynamics* (anxiety-based and unconscious defences).[74] For an arts organisation, leveraging the key covert processes is critical in securing change outcomes, particularly as the staff will likely hold great visionary aspirations for the art form and impact of the organisation. By leveraging these aspirations, it is possible to mobilise change faster than by just relying on logic and analysis.

Lessons from the RSC experience
As I look back over the three years that I have spent with the RSC, I know that the various participatory processes led by key stakeholders (Heywood and Boyd) have mobilised the change journey and have unleashed energy within the organisation. By focusing on the principles of distributed leadership, multiplying imagination, engagement and participation, we employed a methodology more suitable to the RSC than an expert-led, formula-led methodology.

The experience also confirmed once again that when a change process puts people's engagement at the heart of it, using high leverage change methodologies, connecting different parts of the organisation together, working through multiple perspectives, and keeping the whole system together, the change effort sticks. What is more, the process we used enabled most people to voice their doubts and scepticism, which the change leaders could then use as part of the data to adjust the pace and the approach to change.

Finally, by using concrete and defined roles to include more individuals within the RSC into the change project early on, we encouraged people to share their passion and dreams about the organisation. This helped to make the transformation more sustainable. The direct involvement of both top management and some key middle managers and senior leaders in the major interventions provided visible support.

To close, I want to highlight two prime reflections from my work with the RSC.

Three conditions that help to make culture-change easier
My work with the RSC has reminded me that, while culture-change can be complex, it can also be made easier if three conditions exist:

· visible and active role-modelling by key leaders
· an appropriate amount of group reconfiguration
· systemic alignment to bed down the behavioural changes in the cultural fabric of the organisation.

Visible leadership Leaders, especially if they are liked and respected (which Heywood and Boyd are), are critical role models in the change journey. People will want to move in the direction their leader signposts for them, especially when there is a psychological bond between those leaders and the staff. However, personal liking will not alone suffice to make a culture-change stick, there have to be processes that help turn initial compliance into commitment. The example of the RSC shows one way in which this can be achieved: through respected leaders demonstrating personally how, in this case by embracing ensemble behaviour, they achieve successful outcomes. By associating successful outcomes with ensemble behaviour, members of staff were helped to see that the new behaviour was a 'good' way to work and how, through practice, the behaviour gradually became part of the new cultural DNA.

Boyd and Heywood held the culture-change process together by living it, talking about it, using it and demonstrating it. There is no doubt that their visible leadership has helped to shift the culture during the past three years.

Reconfiguration of groups Culture is a dynamic phenomenon that, as well as being shaped by leadership behaviour, is constantly enacted and created by interactions between individuals and groups. In this sense, culture constantly evolves and is shaped through interaction between people. One way to shift culture is therefore by reconfiguring groups within the organisation, mixing up different communities and helping them to interact with each other, creating opportunities for paradigm and reality to be reshaped as different groups influence each other's approach to work. As Edgar Schein of MIT Sloan School of Management puts it, culture happens not so much 'in' people but 'in between' people.[75] Therefore, by modifying the interaction, we modified the texture of group thinking.

System (organisational) alignment to reinforce the behavioural change At the RSC, the great work that the Human Resources and Communications departments did helped to embed the behavioural changes. Adele Cope (Human Resources) and Liz Thompson (Communications) aligned many RSC systems and processes to ensure there was a 'systemic' platform to support the ensemble culture. Many of their impressive efforts have started to pay dividends; I am sure there will be more to come if the RSC continues to work in an ensemble way.

Trust is a key ingredient of effective partnership.
I valued my partnership with Vikki Heywood (who was the key client) because it was mutually supportive and trusting. She knew I could provide the methodological leadership, and I knew she could navigate the complexities of applying the methodology to the specific RSC context. Together, we worked out how to steer change through the complex politics, people's intense emotions, and strong-minded leaders. We also worked out a strategy on how to work separately with other key stakeholders. This was possible because I trusted Vikki's judgement and her 'feel' for the system's dynamics. I also knew that my role as a third party helper was to ensure she was the key driver of this change journey, not me. It is this trust that kept me in the role for three years without a clear brief or a clearly defined role.

For the first time in my professional life, I was engaged in a project in which I had no proper 'contract' from the client – by contract, I do not mean a document that outlines the financial agreement, I mean a document that outlined the scope, scale, nature of the job commissioned, sequence of work, my role, and who were the stakeholder groups that I was expected to liaise with. At times, it was very frustrating – we could have done more if we had more clarity, had been more systematic, and had taken a longer-term view. However, I knew that Heywood had chosen this path because of her in-depth knowledge of the RSC's culture. It was right not to be clear about my 'contract' because the system could only take one step at a time. If I had scoped my role, it would have frightened key stakeholders. Within the RSC's culture, people are reluctant to commit to a 'programmatic' approach to change because they want to think about the next step only after they have seen the results of the first step. I soon learnt that while it was important for me to design and hold the entire change process in my head, I could not publicly commit this to paper. This required trust in those for whom and with whom I work, and their trust in me.

Last word

Working across borders with ease and elegance – an ensemble way of working – is what most organisations should be aiming for. The exchange of perspectives enables organisations to adapt with greater ease. Leaders instinctively know that paradigm agility and seamless collaboration will lead to agile products (productions in the case of RSC) as well as customer service agility. In the tough economic environment currently prevailing, people need to learn how to behave as entrepreneurs by going across borders to secure resources to deliver results that matter to the organisation.

Initially, the process of becoming an ensemble organisation was a value alignment exercise for the RSC. However, I hope the rest of the RSC's leaders will soon come to see the ensemble approach as a way of becoming agile and flexible, to help the RSC thrive in a turbulent environment with diminishing resources. I hope the RSC case encourages many other organisations to take a bold and innovative approach to preparing their organisation for the future.

Thank you Royal Shakespeare Company for giving me this rich learning experience.

Mee-Yan Cheung-Judge, December 2009
Quality and Equality, LTD
www.quality-equality.com

Appendix 1
List of Interviewees

During the course of the project, we conducted over 60 interviews with figures connected with the RSC's present and past. We are grateful to all of the people listed below for the time they spared in speaking to us about the RSC.

Internal interviewees

This is an alphabetical list of members of staff interviewed in the summer of 2007 and again in the summer of 2009. The second wave of interviews included a broader sample from across the organisation, including representatives of other departments as well as those to whom we spoke in 2007. All interviews were conducted on the proviso of anonymity and therefore we have listed names alphabetically and have not indicated who featured in which round of interviews.

The interviews allowed us to assess organisational change within the RSC from individual perspectives but from the point of view of function. In the case of departures or changes of organisational structure, we therefore interviewed successors to roles or the nearest equivalent. Where applicable, this is indicated in the list below.

Pippa Adamson	Chief Management Accountant (succeeded by Irina Gorbunowa in 2008)
Libby Alexander	Training and Development Manager
Sara Aspley	Director of Commercial Services
Alan Bartlett	Head of Construction and Technical Design
Maureen Beattie	Actor (The Histories Ensemble)
Corinne Beaver	London Manager

John Benfield	Head of Digital
Simon Bowler	Head of Engineering Services
Michael Boyd	Artistic Director
Mary Butlin	Head of Market Planning
David Collins	Head of Marketing
Adele Cope	HR Director
Lyn Darnley	Head of Voice and Artistic Development
Grug Davies	Head of Estates
Greg Doran	Chief Associate Director
Liza Frank	Assistant to Artistic Director (succeeded Thea Jones in 2008)
Geoffrey Freshwater	Actor (The Histories Ensemble and the second Long Ensemble)
Irina Gorbunowa	Chief Management Accountant (succeeded Pippa Adamson in 2008)
Jondon Gourkan	Company Manager
Steve Haworth	Head of Sales and Ticketing
Vikki Heywood	Executive Director
Chris Hill	Director of Sales and Marketing
Kate Horton	Commercial Director (left winter 2007, role divided between Sara Aspley and Chris Hill)
Lyndon Jones	Assistant to Executive Office
Thea Jones	Assistant to Artistic Director (left 2008, succeeded by Liza Frank)
James Kitto	front of house Manager
Geoff Locker	Technical Director
Barry Lytollis	Stage Door
Alastair McArthur	Head of Costume
Chris McGill	Actor (The Histories Ensemble)
Beverly Milne	Accounts Officer, Payables
Maria Mottram	Box Office
Chris O'Brien	Head of IT
Jacqui O'Hanlon	Director of Education
Andrew Parker	Director of Finance and Administration
Michele Percy	Assistant to Executive Director
Tom Piper	Associate Designer

Deborah Shaw	Associate Director
Lex Shrapnel	Actor (The Histories Ensemble)
Jonathan Slinger	Actor (The Histories Ensemble)
Audrey Spencer	Estates
Liz Thompson	Director of Communications
Denise Wood	Lead Producer

We are also grateful to members of the acting ensemble company who played *Hamlet*, *A Midsummer Night's Dream* and *Love's Labour's Lost* in autumn 2008, with whom we conducted a discussion group. We are also grateful to the members of the second ensemble who allowed us to observe both their induction in January 2009, and then a rehearsal of *As You Like It* in March 2009.

During the research, we also interviewed several members of staff, both past and present, about specific aspects of the RSC. In the text, these are referenced as dated interviews.

Sir Christopher Bland, Interview, 18 February 2008
Michael Boyd, Interview, 2 June 2009
Mary Butlin, Interview, 29 April 2008
Adele Cope, Interview, 17 July 2008
Adele Cope, Interview 15 June 2009
Sir Peter Hall, Interview, 4 June 2008
Vikki Heywood, Interview, 17 July 2007
Vikki Heywood, Interview, 29 May 2009
Chris Hill, Interview, 16 May 2008
Andrew Parker, Interview, 12 May 2008
Andrew Parker and Adele Cope, Interview, 26 November 2008
Peter Wilson, Interview, 13 January 2009

External interviewees

During the research, we also spoke to people who had either
worked with the RSC in the past, or who have worked with the
organisation recently.

Pippa Adamson	Chief Operating Officer, The Royal Ballet School – (qv internal interviewees) interviewed as a former employee of the RSC
Michael Attenborough	Artistic Director, the Almeida Theatre, former Principal Associate Director, RSC
Kim Evans	Executive Director, Arts, Arts Council England, 1999–2006
Sir Peter Hall	Founder of the RSC
Andy Hayles	Managing Director, Charcoal Blue – theatre consultants on the construction of the RSC's theatres
Charles Leadbeater	Independent consultant, advised the RSC at the time of Project Fleet
Prof. Kate McCluskie	Director, Shakespeare Institute, University of Birmingham
Prof. Stanley Wells	Former director of the Shakespeare Institute at the University of Birmingham and former member of the RSC board

Appendix 2
The Royal Shakespeare Company

As of December 2009, the RSC listed its members in programmes and annual reports as follows.

Patron
Her Majesty the Queen
President
His Royal Highness the Prince of Wales
Deputy President
Sir Geoffrey Cass

Board
Chairman – Sir Christopher Bland
Professor Jonathan Bate, CBE FBA FRSL
Artistic Director – Michael Boyd
Damon Buffini
David Burbidge OBE
Jane Drabble OBE
Noma Dumezweni
Mark Foster
Gilla Harris
Executive Director — Vikki Heywood
John Hornby
Jonathan Kestenbaum
Paul Morrell OBE
Tim Pigott-Smith
Neil Rami
Deputy Chairman – Lady Sainsbury of Turville

Governors
George Alagiah OBE
Yasmin Alibhai-Brown
Professor Jonathan Bate, CBE FBA FRSL
Jana Bennett
Malorie Blackman OBE
Sir Christopher Bland
Lee C. Bollinger
Michael Boyd
Damon Buffini
David Burbidge OBE
Lord Carter of Barnes CBE
Sir Geoffrey Cass
Sinead Cusack

Elizabeth Dixon
Jane Drabble OBE
Noma Dumezweni
Sir Brian Follett
Mark Foster
Gilla Harris
Vikki Heywood
John Hornby
Laurence Isaacson CBE
Jonathan Kestenbaum
Ian Laing CBE
Sir Michael Lyons
Paul Morrell OBE
David Oyelowo
Charlotte Heber Percy
Tim Pigott-Smith
Neil Rami
Lisa Houghton Reade
Ian Ritchie CBE, RA
Rosemary Said
Wafic Said
Lady Sainsbury of Turville
Brockman Seawell
David Suchet OBE
Meera Syal MBE
Michael Wood

Honorary Emeritus Governors
Lady Anderson
Charles Flower
Drue Heinz DBE
Frederick R. Koch
Leonard Mathews OBE
Professor Stanley Wells CBE

Honorary Governors
Robert Anthoine
Philip Bermingham
Michael Crystal QC
Tony Hales CBE

Artistic and Associate Director's Office
Artistic Director – Michael Boyd
Chief Associate Director – Gregory Doran
Associate Directors – David Farr, Rupert
Goold, Deborah Shaw, Roxana Silbert
Artistic Associate – Kathryn Hunter
Literary Associate – Anthony Neilson
Associate Designer – Tom Piper
Assistant to the Assoc. Director – Helen Pollock
Assistant to the Artistic Director – Jane Tassell

Assistant Directors
Justin Audibert
Michael Fentiman
Leonie Kubigsteltig
Helen Leblique
Michael Longhurst
Vik Sivalingam

Automation
Head Of Automation – Eric Dixon
Automation Technician – Richard Sharp
Senior Automation Technicians – Ben Leefe
Haydn Wright
Acting Head Of Automation – Richard Smith

Casting
Casting Assistant – Jim Arnold
Head of Casting – Hannah Miller
Casting Director – Helena Palmer
Assistant Casting Director – Janine Snape

Honorary Chaplain
Revd Martin Gorick

Cleaners and Porters
Paula Adlem
David Allcock
Rod Barnet
Nanezda Cirule
Elizabeth Clifford
Lisa Cowley
Alison Hannabus
David Hannabus
Robert Holloway
Yvonne Hudman
Rosemary Payne
Valerie Potts
Joanna Skwara
Mary Smart
Joanna Szymanska
Bill Taylor
Mark Usher
Graham Wright

Barry Maguire
David Rowland
Michael Truscott
Porters Team Leader – Julian Lines
Senior Porter – Gerald Wheeldon

Commercial
Director Of Commercial Services –
Sara Aspley
Director of Sales and Marketing – Chris Hill
*Assistant to Director of Commercial
Services and Director of Sales and
Marketing* – Julia Lister

Company and Stage Management
Company Managers – Michael Dembowicz
Jondon
Kt Vine
Stage Managers – Suzi Blakey
Suzanne Bourke
Nafeesah Butt
Robbie Cullen
Pip Horobin
Deputy Stage Managers – Alison Daniels
Nicola Ireland
Heidi Lennard
Klare Roger
Gabrielle Sanders
Juliette Taylor
Assistant Stage Managers – Jemma
Carpenter
Christie Gerrard
Amy Griffin
Katie Hutcheson
Joanna Vimpany

Costume
Temporary Costume Department
Administrator – Delfina Angiolini
*First Assistant (Mens) (Maternity
Cover)* – Rosie Armitage
Head of Dye – Helen Baines
Head of Ladies' Costume – Isabelle Comte
*Skilled Dye Technician (Maternity
Cover)* – Jenny Cowgill
Skilled Costumiers (Ladies) – Sarah Collins
Helen Davenport
Deborah Jaunai-Recardo
*Costume Department
Administrator* – Ivan Douglas
Principal Ladies Cutter – Denise Edwards
Senior Dye Technician – Rebecca Edwards
Skilled Costumiers (Mens) – Susie England
Hannah Mcdermott

First Milliners - Kate Freshwater
Sarah Plowright
Head of Footwear and Armoury - Julian Gilbert
Senior Costumiers (Mens) - Brenda Gollnast
Jane Rogalski
Head of Men's Costume - Emma Harrup
First Dye Technician - Charlotte Hobbs
First Costumier (Ladies) - Esther Hunter
Principal Men's Cutter - Natalie Kurzcewski
Stock Keeper - Sally Locke
First Costumier (Mens) - Yvette Manhood
Head of Costume - Alistair McArthur
Assistant Costume Supervisor - Zarah
Meherali
Head of Hats and Jewellery - Elaine Moore
Senior Leatherworker - Alan Smith
First Footwear Technician - Jessica Smith
Senior Milliner - Margaret Wakelin
Stock Keeper/Buyer - Veronika
Weidenhiller

Costume Hire
Costume Hire Administrator -
Charlene Land
Costume Hire Assistants -
Julia Drummond-Haig
Rosie Miller
Stephanie Smith
Anna Taylor
Head of Costume Hire - Alison Mitchell

Design
Trainee Designer - Katie Lias

Development
Events and Stewardship
Manager - Helen Cave
Development and Planning Officer
- Matthew Collins
Development Co-ordinator -
Michele Cottiss
Individual Giving Manager - Joe Foulsham
Annual Fund Co-Ordinator - Julie Harris
Research Officer - Chris Johnson
Director Of Development - Caroline Jones
Senior Major Gifts Manager - Catherine
Kernot
Trusts Manager - Hamble Padden
Major Gifts Officer - Andrew Rye
Acting Head of Annual Fund - Carol
Stevenson
Campaign Co-Ordinator - Lauren Thorpe
Research Manager - Louise Turner
Corporate Partnerships Manager

- Angela Vellender
Deputy Development Director - Graeme
Williamson

Drawing Office
Head of Construction & Technical
Design - Alan Bartlett
Design Engineers - Nicholas Bell,
David Harris
Senior Draughtspeople - David Jones,
Charles MacCall
Draughtsperson - Brett Weatherhead

Duty Managers
Nicky Cox
Suzanne Harris
James Kitto
Sheelagh Saunders

Education
Administrator, Capital Centre Post
Graduate Programmes - Amanda Carroll
Project Manager, School
Partnerships - Fiona Clayton
Head of School Partnerships - Rob Elkington
Administrator, Young People's
Programme - Rob Freeman
Lead Practitioner - Virginia Grainger
Project Manager London, Young People's
Programme - Sonia Hyams
Head of Young People's
Programme - Fiona Ingram
Project Manager, School
Partnerships - Tracy Irish
Assistant to the Director of
Education - Sarah Keevill
Acting Head of Young People's
Programme - Jamie Luck
Director of Education - Jacqueline O'Hanlon
Administrator, School
Partnerships - Sheila O'Sullivan
Project Manager, Young People's
Programme - Liisa Spink
Department Manager - Melanie Whitehead
E-Learning Manager - Kate Wolstenholme

Engineering Services
Head of Engineering Services - Simon Bowler
Maintenance Electrician - Mark Farmer
Administrative Assistant - Tim Oliver
Senior Maintenance Electrician
- Richard Power
Electrical Test Technician - Martin Simms

Enterprise
Enterprise Assistant – Lucy Barriball
Programmes Co-ordinator – Michelle Morton
Commercial Manager – Kevin Wright

Estates
Sue Allen
Nancy Cooper
*Chapel Lane Reception Officer
(Evening)* – Denise Hagon
Postal Assistants – Nanezda Cirule
Ann Kelly
Access Manager – Pat Collcutt
Director of Estates – Grug Davies
Properties Manager – Suzanne Harris
PA to the Director of Estates – Suzanne
Jones
Sally Luntley
*Chapel Lane Reception Officer
(Daytime)* – Gemma Vowles
Fire Officer – Christopher Oliver
Estates Administrator – Audrey Spencer
Senior Fire Office – Paul Tursner-Upcott
Interim Facilities Manager – Wendy
Woodcock

Events & Exhibitions
*Director of Events &
Exhibitions* – Geraldine Collinge
Events Assistant – Nicky Cox
*Curator of RSC Collection &
Archive* – David Howells
*Assistant to the Director of Events &
Exhibitions* – Helen Pollock
Curatorial Assistant – Caroline Ray
*Curatorial Assistant (Maternity
Cover)* – Rosalyn Smith
Events & Exhibitions Co-ordinator –
Jo Whitford

Executive Director's Office
Executive Director – Vikki Heywood
PA to the Executive Office – Lyndon
Jones
*Assistant to the Executive Director &
Clerk to the Governors* – Michele Percy

Finance
Project Finance Manager – Anna
Anderson
Pensions & Insurance Officer – Ron
Codrington
Accounts Services Officers – Linda Lloyd
Bev Milne

Joyce Natzler
Theresa York
Payroll Officer – Adrian Gelston
Senior Management Accountant – Irina
Gorbunowa
Payroll Manager – Becky Harris
Management Accountants – Anthea
Dauncey
Catherine Greenway *(Maternity Cover)*
Chris Harris
Doreen Massey
Beth Payne
Ben Waters
Internal Auditor – Sarah Hedgecock
Director of Finance & Administration
– Andrew Parker
Financial Services Manager – Mike White
Accounts Services Manager – Andrew
Woodward

Front of House
Ushers – James Allan
Annette Ashfield
Toby Barnett
Margaret Bidgood
Hege Bleidvin-Sandaker
Kathleen Bradley
Hayley Burgess
Jocelyn Carter
Lucy Chandler
Lorraine Deller
Ellen Frost
Susan Harris
Yvonne Harris
Ann Kelly
Ben Luntley
Hilary Lynch
Carol Morris
Alan Robson
Nicola Salmon
Dennis Southall
Mary Taylor
Fiona Tursner-Upcott
Susan Whatmore
Linda Wimperis
*Audience Care and Tours
Administrator* – Holly Clarke
Attendants – Claire-Louise Cairns
Roy Holton
David Wimperis
Front of House Manager – James Kitto
Head of Audience Care – Elizabeth
Wainwright

Gardeners
Head Gardener - Robert Holt

Graphic Design
Graphic Designer - Clare Booth
Artworker - Matthew Boss
Senior Graphic Designer - Sophie Clausen
Print Buyer & Graphics
Coordinator - Gina Print
Head of Graphic Design - Andy Williams

Green Room
Catering Assistants - Sarah Furniss
Carole Sambrook-Hurst
Veronica Treharne
Green Room Supervisor - Sylvia Hall
Catering Manager - Ruth Treharne

Health & Safety
Health & Safety Administrative
Assistant - Hayley Burgess
Health & Safety Advisor - Gail Miller
Technical/Health & Safety Training
Coordinator - Jo Young

Human Resources
Training and Development
Manager - Libby Alexander
HR Administrator - Rachel Barnes
Director of Human Resources - Adele Cope
Training & Development Assistant - Lucy
Gregory
Assistant HR Manager - Jessica Harris
Training & Development Officer - Gavin
Horsfall
HR Manager - Darrell Mitchell
PA to HR Director - Elizabeth Nicholson
Occupational Health Advisor - Shirley
Prenton-Jones
HR Officer - Davinder Sandhu

IT
Database Developer - Robin Astle
Administrator - Debby Bailey
Systems Manager - Wayne Evans
Systems Developer - Lee Fear
Support Services Manager - Jacqui Hamp
Tessitura Co-ordinator and Development
Manager - Ruth Harris
Web Developer - Alex Kirkwood
IT Support Specialists - John Mills
Paul Willett
Head of Information Technology - Chris
O'Brien

Network Manager - Matthew Reading

Legal
General Counsel - Caroline Barnett
PA to the General Counsel - Emma Welch

Lighting
Special Senior Lighting
Technicians - Caroline Burrell
Keith Cookson
Simon Spencer
First Lighting Technicians - Jake Brain
Kevin Carson
Tim Owen
Mathew Peel
David Richardson
Lighting Technician - Lauren Watson
Creative & Visual Media Technician - Tim
Baxter
Jason Hackett
Maxwell White
Assistant Head of Lighting - Simon
Bayliss
Head of RSC Lighting - Vince Herbert

Literary Department
Literary Manager - Pippa Hill
RSC/Capital International Playwright In
Residence - Tarell Alvin McCraney
Company Dramaturg - Jeanie O'Hare

London Operations
Clapham Caretakers - Carl Allen
Wendy Turnstill
London Manager - Corinne Beaver
London Administration
Assistant - Lauren Rubery

Maintenance
Maintenance Painter & Decorator -
Clive Bardell
Maintenance Assistant - Steve Cross
Maintenance Manager - Bill Rostron

Marketing
Marketing Officer (Corporate) - Amy Clarke
Head of Marketing - David Collins
Marketing Officer
(Productions) - Natasha Goodge
Assistant Marketing Officer
(Corporate) - Elin Joseph
Marketing Manager (Corporate) - Jo Litt
Marketing Manager (Productions) - Anna
Mitchelson

Market Planning

Head of Market Planning – Mary Butlin

Movement

Manager, Movement – Jane Hazell
Head of Movement – Struan Leslie

Music

Music Manager – Kate Andrew
Music Assistant – Sarah Balls
Musicians – James Jones
Kevin Pitt
Ian Reynolds
David Statham
Andrew Stone Fewings
Music Director – Bruce O'Neil
Music Co-ordinator – Richard Sandland
Head of Music – John Woolf

Nursery

Nursery Assistant – Laura Cameron
Nursery Practioners – Victoria Alcock
Kate Clifford
Ewelina Figlewska
Dawn Francis
Elizabeth Knowlton
James Pavitt
June Prickett
Delphine Saul
Yolana Wassersug
Deputy Head of Nursery – Christine Green
Deputy Head of Nursery – Yvonne
Robbins
Head of Nursery – Kate Robinson
Nursery Administrator – Bobbie Schofield

Communications

Press and Communications Officer – Dean
Asker
Head of Digital Media – John Benfield
Communications Assistant – Lucy Billiard
Web Editor – Clea Boorman
Communications Assistant – Kathleen
Bradley
Communications Manager – Jane Ellis
Assistant Digital Media Producer – Fiona
Handscomb
Head of Press – Philippa Harland
*PA to Director of
Communications* – Lucien Riviere
Director of Communications – Liz Thompson
Press & Marketing Assistant – Alex Turner
Digital Media Producer – Suzanne
Worthington

Senior Press Officer – Nada Zakula

Producers

Producers – Jeremy Adams
Kevin Fitzmaurice
Touring Administrator – Rachael Barber
Assistant Producers – Gareth Collins
Zoë Donegan
Planning Co-ordinators – Victoria Picken
Rachel Wall
Assistant to the Producers – Mardi
Widdowson
Lead Producer – Denise Wood

Production Office

Senior Production Managers – Simon Ash
Mark Graham
Deputy Technical Director – Peter Bailey
Technical Manager – Julian Cree
Production Managers – Peter Griffin
Rebecca Watts
Technical Director – Geoff Locker
PA to Technical Director – Elizabeth
Nicholson
Assistant Production Manager – David
Tanqueray
Staff Scheduling Co-ordinator – Alun Thomas

Project Office

Project Co-ordinator – Belinda Aird
Deputy Project Director – Simon Harper
Project Office Manager – Katie Martin
Technical Project Co-ordinator – Flip Tanner
Project Co-ordinator – Harry Teale
Project Director – Peter Wilson

Property Workshop

Prop Technicians – Maggie Atkins
Malcolm Brain
Carl Taylor
Mel West
Head of Property Workshop – John Evans
Assistant Prop Technician – Rufus
McDermot
*Property Workshop
Apprentice* – Christopher Simmonds

Retail

Shops Sales Assistants – Ann Barnicoat
Lynne Dunningham
Jennifer Farmer
Stores Senior Supervisor – Alan Chandler
Senior Sales Assistants – Sheila Day
Gwen Rogers
Merchandiser – Pippa Green
Mail Order Senior Supervisor – Sarah Holt

Retail Development Manager – Sarah Lovsey
Shops Senior Supervisor – Biddy Wilson

Running Wardrobe

Deputy Wardrobe Mistress – Jennifer Binns
Wardrobe Mistress – Carolyn Daniels
Dressers – Yvonne Gilbert
Keith Lovell
Michael Nolan
Linda Williams
Assistant Wardrobe Mistress – Josie Horton
Relief Dresser – Keiko Spencer

Sales And Ticketing

Sales Manager (Productions) – Patricia Boycott
Sales Operators – Yolanda Cross
Christine Elliott
Emma Fleming
Susan Gardner
Elizabeth Gill
Norma Henderson
Margaret Jackson
David Mears
Chris Morgan
Maria Mottram
Elizabeth Rawlinson
Ellen Reade
Jane Trotman
Marilyn Walton
Finance Assistant – Esther Gillman
Sales Manager (Operations) – Kim Goodman
Head of Sales and Ticketing – Steve Haworth
Sales Operators (Support) – Pauline Humphrey
Dolores Manteiga Defente
Kerry-Sue Peplow
Sales Manager (Systems) – Gerry Martin
Membership Assistant – Loraine Mitchell
Membership Secretary – Sally Nortcliffe
Administration Assistant – Samantha Thompson-Taylor

Scenic Art

Head of Scenic Art – Rebecca Ashley
Third Assistant Scenic Artist – Stephanie Kinsella
Paintshop Apprentice – Paul Riddle
Scenic Artist – Joe Vassallo
Senior Scenic Artist – Alice Watkins

Scenic Engineering

Scenic Engineers – Daren Ainsworth
Phil Malins
Jacob Robbins
Martin Robinson
Senior Engineers – Kevin Neville
Ian Rhind
Assistant Engineer – Lewis Pierpoint
Deputy Scenic Engineering Manager – Tobias Robbins
Scenic Engineering Manager – David Tinson

Scenic Workshop

Senior Scenic Carpenters – Richard Brain
Julian Crang
David Dewhurst
David Watson
Carpenters – Andrew Clark
Matthew Jacques
Ross Kitching
Gavin Reeves
Assistant Machinist – Paul Collins
Will Fagan
Scenic Workshop Apprentice – Sam Reynolds
Scenic Workshop Manager – Paul Hadland
Deputy Scenic Manager – James Hicks
Logistics Manager – Robert Hinton
Scenic Carpenter – Benjamin Morris
Deputy Scenic Manager – Brian Robbins
Storeman – Roger South
Scenic Assistant – John Speakman

Sound

Sound Technician – Michelle Davies
First Sound Technicians – Claire Carroll
Andrew Franks
Jonathan Ruddick
Chris Vernon
Senior Sound Technicians – Mike Compton
Martin Slavin
Head of Sound – Jeremy Dunn

Stage

Stage Technicians – Matt Aston
Tom Horton
Steve Keeley
Tom Mellon
Simon Packer
Grant Skidmore
Kevin Wimperis
Specialised Senior Technician – Darren

Guy
Senior Stage Technicians – Mark Collins
Alistair Pitts
Tom Watts
Stage Supervisor – Roger Haymes

Stage Door
Stage Door Keepers – Sue Allen
Patricia Carnell
Denise Hagon
Sandra Holt
Barry Lytollis
Shirley Penderell-Goodricke
Nightwatch Officers – David E Jones
Michael Truscott

Text And Voice
Director of Text and Voice – Cicely Berry
Senior Text and Voice Coach – Alison
Bomber
Voice Placement – Charlie D'aeth
*Head of Text, Voice & Artist
Development* – Lyn Darnley
*Manager, Text, Voice & Artist
Development* – Jane Hazell

Wigs & Make-Up
*Assistant Wig & Make-Up
Artists* – Kimberley Boyce
Kirsten Job
Wig & Make-Up Artists – Lavinia Blackwell
Sindy Cooper
Fiona Keston
Senior Wig & Make-Up Artists – Charlotte
Griffiths
Rachel Seal
*Wigs & Make-Up Department
Supervisor* – Sandra Smith

Actors

During the period covered by this report, we were able to speak to and observe the work of three acting ensembles. Their members are listed below as they were listed in the RSC's programmes and annual reports for this period.

The Histories Ensemble

Nicholas Asbury
Hannah Barrie
Keith Bartlett
Maureen Beattie
Antony Bunsee
Rob Carroll
Matt Costain
Julius D'Silva
Keith Dunphy
Wela Frasier
Geoffrey Freshwater
Paul Hamilton
Alexia Healy
Kieran Hill
Tom Hodgkins
Chuk Iwuji
John MacKay
Forbes Masson
Chris McGill
Patrice Naiambana
Luke Neil
Sandy Neilson
Ann Ogombo
Miles Richardson
Lex Shrapnel
Anthony Shuster
Jonathan Slinger
Katy Stephens
Geoffrey Streatfield
James Tucker
David Warner
Roger Watkins
Clive Wood

The Hamlet/Dream Ensemble

David Ajala
Sam Alexander
Edward Bennett
Ricky Champ
Ewen Cummins
Robert Curtis
Tom Davey
Peter de Jersey
Joe Dixon
Penny Downie
Kathryn Drysdale
Samuel Dutton
Oliver Ford Davies
Ryan Gage
Mariah Gale
Mark Hadfield
Andrea Harris
Jim Hooper
Keith Osborn
Roderick Smith
Nina Sosanya
Riann Steele
Sir Patrick Stewart
David Tennant
Zoe Thorne
Natalie Walter
John Woodvine

The Long Ensemble

Charles Aitken
Joseph Arkley
Adam Burton
David Carr
Brian Doherty
Darrell D'Silva
Noma Dumezweni
Dyfan Dwyfor
Phillip Edgerley
Christine Entwhistle
Geoffrey Freshwater
James Gale
Mariah Gale
Gruffudd Glynn
Paul Hamilton
Greg Hicks
James Howard
Kathryn Hunter
Kelly Hunter
Ansu Kabia
Tunji Kasim
Richard Katz
Debbie Korley
John Mackay
Forbes Masson
Sandy Neilson
Jonjo O'Neill
Dharmesh Patel
Peter Peverley
Patrick Romer
David Rubin
Sophie Russell
Oliver Ryan
Simone Saunders
Peter Shorey
Clarence Smith
Katy Stephens
James Traherne
Sam Troughton
James Tucker
Larrington Walker
Kirsty Woodward
Hannah Young
Samantha Young

Notes

1   See Holbeche, *The High Performance Organisation: Creating dynamic stability and sustainable success.*

2   Mintzberg, *Harvard Business Review,* Jul–Aug 2009, p142.

3   Ibid, p140.

4   Arts Council, *Appraisal Report: Royal Shakespeare Company*, p7.

5   Boyd, 'Playing our proper role: the way forward for the Royal Shakespeare Company', p4.

6   Baracaia, *Stage*, 14 Feb 2002; Benedict, *Observer*, 31 Mar 2002; Billington, *Guardi*an, 6 Mar2002.

7   Baracaia, *Stage,* 14 Feb 2002.

8   RSC, 'RSC purpose and values'.

9   Boyd, 'Playing our proper role.' p2.

10 Boyd, speech at the New York Public Library

11 Ibid.

12 RSC, *Strategic Plan 2006-2012: Mapping the journey for the Royal Shakespeare Company to 2012*, p11.

13 RSC, *130th Annual Report 2006/07*, p4.

14 Boyd interview 2009.

15   Ibid.

16   Boyd, 'Playing our proper role', p4.

17   RSC, *129th Annual Report 2004/05*, p7.

18   See Zuboff and Maxmin, *The Support Economy: Why corporations are failing individuals and the next stage of capitalism.*

19   See Leadbeater, *Personalisation Through Participation.*

20   See Shirky, *Here Comes Everybody: The power of organising without organisations*; and Leadbeater, *We-Think: Mass innovation not mass production: The power of mass creativity.*

21   Boyd, speech at the New York Public Library.

22   Hall interview 2008.

23   Heywood interview 2007.

24   Bland interview 2009.

25   Ibid.

26   RSC, *Strategic Plan 2006-2012: Mapping the journey for the Royal Shakespeare Company to 2012*, p28.

27   Heywood interview 2007.

28   RSC, *Strategic Plan 2006-2012: Mapping the journey for the Royal Shakespeare Company to 2012*, p24.

29   Asbury, *Exit Pursued by a Badger: An actor's journey through history with Shakespeare*, p29.

30   Boyd interview 2009.

31 Bland interview 2009.

32 Spencer, *Telegraph*, 18 Apr 2008

33 Hill interview 2008.

34 Parker interview 2008.

35 Borgatti et al, *Ucinet for Windows: software for social network analysis.*

36 Krackhardt and Hanson, *How organisations win by working together*, p104.

37 Shirky, *Here Comes Everybody: The power of organising without organisations*, pp39–40.

38 Heywood interview 2009.

39 Boyd interview 2009.

40 Neelands et al., *An Evaluation of Stand Up for Shakespeare – The Royal Shakespeare Company Learning and Performance Network 2006-2009*, p6.

41 Ibid, p7.

42 Ibid, p9.

43 Ibid, p74.

44 GfK NOP, *RSC Company Survey 2009.*

45 MacLeod and Clark, *Engaging for Success: Enhancing performance through employee engagement*, p3.

46 Eatwell, 'Economic outlook', *Chartered Management Institutute*, p5.

47   Boyd interview 2009.

48   Ibid.

49   Ibid.

50   Heywood interview 2009.

51   Boyd interview 2009.

52   See Leadbeater and Oakley, *The Independents: Britain's new cultural entrepreneurs.*

53   Bass and Stogdill, *Handbook of Leadership: A survey of theory and research.*

54   See Peters and Waterman, *In Search of Excellence*; and Collins and Porras, *Built to Last: Succesful habits of visionary companies.*

55   See Battelle, *Search: How Google and its rivals rewrote the rules of business and transformed our culture.*

56   Boyd, speech at the New York Public Library.

57   Simms, *The Director*, Jun 2009.

58   Holbeche, *The High Performance Organisation: Creating dynamic stability and sustainable success*, p8.

59   Mintzberg, *Harvard Business Review,* Jul–Aug 2009, p142.

60   See Sennett, *The Craftsman*; and Malone, *The Future of Work: How the new order of business will shape your organisation, your management style, and your life.*

61   Skidmore, 'Leading between', p100.

62 Holbeche, *The High Performance Organisation: Creating dynamic stability and sustainable success*, p12.

63 Catmull, 'Interview with Iinnovate'.

64 Holbeche, *The High Performance Organisation: Creating dynamic stability and sustainable success*, p6.

65 Hewison, *Not a Sideshow: Leadership and cultural value*, p43.

66 Zeleny, *New York Times*, 9 Nov 2008

67 George, *7 Lessons for Leading in Crisis*, p75.

68 RSC, press release, 8 Dec 2008.

69 Economist Intelligence Unit, *Securing the Value of Business Process Change*.

70 See Weisbord, *Organisational Diagnosis: A workbook of theory and practice*.

71 See Holman and Devane, *The Change Handbook: Group methods for shaping the future*.

72 Bunker and Alban, *Large Group Interventions: Engaging the whole system for rapid change*; and Wheatley, *Leadership and The New Science: Discovering the order in a chaotic world*.

73 Bridges, *Managing Transitions: Making the most of change*.

74 Marshak, *Covert processes at work*.

75 Schein, *The Corporate Culture Survival Guide*.

Bibliography

Arts Council, *Appraisal Report: Royal Shakespeare Company*, typescript (London: Arts Council, 1990).

Asbury, N, *Exit Pursued by a Badger: An actor's journey through history with Shakespeare* (London: Oberon Books, 2009).

Baracaia, A, 'West affirms RSC criticism', *The Stage,* 14 Feb 2002.

Bass, BM and Stogdill, RM, *Handbook of Leadership: A survey of theory and research* (New York: The Free Press, 1990).

Battelle, J, *Search: How Google and its rivals rewrote the rules of business and transformed our culture* (London and New York: Penguin, 2005).

Beauman, S, *Royal Shakespeare Company: A history of ten decades* (Oxford: Oxford University Press, 1982).

Benedict, D, 'Is the RSC safe in his hands?', *Observer,* 31 Mar 2002.

Billington, M, 'Something rotten in Stratford', *Guardian,* 6 Mar 2002.

Bloom, N and Van Reenen, J, 'Measuring and explaining management practices across firms and countries', Centre for Economic Performance discussion paper No. 176 (London: LSE, 2006).

Borgatti, SP, Everett, MG and Freeman, LC, *Ucinet for Windows: software for social network analysis* (Harvard, MA: Analytic Technologies, 2002).

Boyd, M, 'Building relationships', *The Stage,* 10–11, 2 April 2009.

Boyd, M, 'Playing our proper role: the way forward for the Royal Shakespeare Company', typescript, Oct 2003.

Boyd, M, speech at the New York Public Library, 20 Jun 2008.

Bridges, W, *Managing Transitions: Making the most of change* (New York: Da Capo Press, 2003).

Bryan, L and Joyce, C, 'The twenty-first century organisation', *McKinsey Quarterly, No. 3,* (2005).

Bunker, BB and Alban, BT, *Large Group Interventions: Engaging the whole system for rapid change* (San Francisco: Jossey Bass, 1996).

Castells, M, *The Rise of the Network Society* (Oxford: Blackwell, 1996).

Catmull, E, 'Interview with Iinnovate', a podcast by students of Stanford University's Business and Design Schools, available at http://iinnovate.blogspot.com/2007/02/dr-ed-catmull-co-founder-and-president.html (accessed 2 Mar 2010).

Chambers, C, Inside the Royal Shakespeare Company (London: Routledge, 2004).

Chief Executive (2008) www.chiefexecutive.net/ME2/dirmod. asp?sid=&nm=&type=Publishing&mod=Publications per cent3A per cent3AArticle&mid=8F3A7027421841978F18BE895 F87F791&id=FD0F481A1CA94DAB9B37216C2EA15F28&tier=4 (accessed 24 Sep 2009)

Collins, J (1995) www.jimcollins.com/article_topics/articles/ building-companies.html (accessed 19 Jan 2010).

Collins, J and Porras, J, 'Building your company's vision', *Harvard Business Review,* 74 (1996).

Collins, J and Porras, J, *Built to Last: Succesful habits of visionary companies* (London: Harper Business, 1994).

Craig, J (ed), *Production Values* (London: Demos, 2006).

Demos, Getting it Together. *The RSC and Ensemble: Feasibility stage report* (London: Demos, 2007).

Eatwell, J, 'Economic outlook', *Chartered Management Institute,* issue 2, Oct 2009.

Economist Intelligence Unit, *Securing the value of business process change,* a study commissioned by Logica Management Consulting, 2008.

George, B, *7 Lessons for Leading in Crisis* (San Francisco: Jossey-Bass, 2009).

GfK NOP, *RSC Company Survey 2009* (London: GFK NOP: 2009).

Gill, P, *Apprenticeship* (London: Oberon Books, 2008).

Goleman, D, *Emotional Intelligence: Why it can matter more than IQ* (London: Bloomsbury, 1996).

Hall, P, *Making an Exhibition of Myself: The autobiography of Sir Peter Hall* (London: Sinclair-Stevenson, 1993).

Heifetz, R, *Leadership Without Easy Answers* (Cambridge, MA: Bellknap Press, 1994).

Hewison, R, *Not a Sideshow: Leadership and cultural value* (London: Demos, 2006).

Holbeche, L, *The High Performance Organisation: Creating dynamic stability and sustainable success* (Oxford: Elsevier Butterworth Heinemann, 2007).

Holden, J, *Cultural Value and the Crisis of Legitimacy* (London: Demos, 2006).

Holden, J, *Democratic Culture* (London, Demos, 2008).

Holman, P and Devane, T, *The Change Handbook: Group methods for shaping the future* (San Francisco: Berrett Koehler, 1999).

Huxham, C and Vangen, S, *Managing to Collaborate: The theory and practice of collaborative advantage* (Abingdon and New York: Routledge, 2005).

Ivey, B, Arts, Inc., *How Greed and Neglect have Destroyed our Cultural Rights* (Berkeley and Los Angeles: University of California Press, 2008).

Jones, S, 'The New Cultural Professionals' in J Craig (ed), *Production Values* (London: Demos, 2006).

Jones, S (ed), *Expressive Lives* (London: Demos, 2009).

Krackhardt, D and Hanson, J, 'Informal networks: the company behind the chart', *Harvard Business Review,* Jul–Aug 1993.

Lank, E, *Collaborative Advantage: How organisations win by working together* (Basingstoke: Palgrave Macmillan, 2005).

Leadbeater, C, *Personalisation Through Participation* (London: Demos, 2004).

Leadbeater, C, *We-Think: Mass innovation not mass production: The power of mass creativity* (London: Profile Books, 2008).

Leadbeater, C and Oakley, K, *The Independents: Britain's new cultural entrepreneurs* (London: Demos, 1999).

MacLeod, D and Clarke, N, *Engaging for Success: Enhancing performance through employee engagement* (London: Department for Business, Innovation and Skills, 2009).

McCarthy, H, Miller, P, and Skidmore, P (eds), *Network Logic* (London: Demos, 2004).

McMaster, B, *Supporting Excellence in the Arts: From measurement to judgement* (London: Department for Culture, Media and Sport, 2008).

Malone, T, *The Future of Work: How the new order of business will shape your organisation, your management style, and your life* (Cambridge, MA: Harvard University Press, 2004).

Marshak, RJ, *Covert processes at work* (San Francisco: Berrett Koehle, 2006).

Miller, P and Skidmore, P, *Disorganisation: Why future organisations must 'loosen up'* (London: Demos, 2004).

Mills, E, 'Newsmaker: meet Google's culture tsar', *CNet News,* 27 Apr 2007, available at http://news.cnet.com/Meet-Googles-culture-czar/2008-1023_3-6179897.html (accessed 2 Mar 2010).

Mintzberg, H, 'Rebuilding companies as communities', *Harvard Business Review,* Jul–Aug 2009.

Mulgan, G, *Connexity: Responsibility, freedom, business and power in the new century* (London: Vintage, 1998).

Neelands, J, Galloway, S and Lindsay, G, *An Evaluation of Stand Up for Shakespeare – The Royal Shakespeare Company Learning and Performance Network 2006-2009* (Warwick: University of Warwick, 2009).

Nye, J, *The Powers to Lead* (Oxford: Oxford University Press, 2008).

O'Leary, D (ed), *The Politics of Public Behaviour* (London: Demos, 2008).

Peters, T and Waterman, R, *In Search of Excellence* (London: Profile Books, 2004).

Power, M, *The Audit Society: Rituals of verification* (Oxford: Oxford University Press, 1997).

Ragsdale, D, 'Surviving the culture change', speech to the Australia Council Summit, Melbourne, 3 Jul 2008, available at http://www.australiacouncil.gov.au/news/speeches/speech_items/diane_ragsdale_address_to_australia_council_arts_marketing_summit (accessed 3 Mar 2010).

Rock, S, 'The Art of Management', *The Manager,* Summer 2008.

RSC, *129th Annual Report 2004/05* (Stratford-upon-Avon: RSC, 2005).

RSC, *130th Annual Report 2006/07* (Stratford-upon-Avon: RSC, 2007).

RSC, 'Board and committee structure and processes of the RSC', typescript, version approved by board on 22 May 2007.

RSC, 'Business Plan version 3', [version 1 created July], typescript, 16 Oct 2001.

RSC, press release, 8 Dec 2008.

RSC, 'RSC purpose and values', typescript, 2008.

RSC, *Strategic Plan 2006-2012: Mapping the journey for the Royal Shakespeare Company to 2012,* typescript, version 1, issued Aug 2006.

RSC, *The Complete Works Yearbook* (Stratford-upon-Avon: RSC, 2007).

Schein, EH, *The Corporate Culture Survival Guide* (San Francisco: Jossey-Bass, 1999).

Senge, P, *The Fifth Discipline: The art and practice of the learning organisation* (New York: Doubleday, 2006).

Sennett, R, *The Craftsman* (London: Allen Lane, 2008).

Shirky, C, *Here Comes Everybody: The power of organising without organisations* (London: Penguin, 2008).

Simms, J, 'Casting a spell', *The Director*, June 2009, available at www.director.co.uk/MAGAZINE/2009/6%20June/ simms_62_11.html.

Skidmore, P, 'Leading between' in H McCarthy et al., (eds), *Network Logic*, (London: Demos, 2004).

Spencer, C, 'Shakespeare's Histories the best I have seen in thirty years', *Daily Telegraph,* 18 Apr 2008.

Stabiner, K, *Inventing Desire: Inside Chiat/Day: The hottest shop, the coolest players, the big business of advertising* (New York: Simon & Schuster, 1993).
Smit, T, *Eden* (London: Bantam Press, 2001).

Taylor, WC and LaBarre, P, 'How Pixar adds a new school of thought to Disney', *The New York Times,* 29 January 2006.

Weisbord, M, *Organisational Diagnosis: A workbook of theory and practice* (Reading, MA: Basic Books, 1978).

Wells, S, *Shakespeare: A dramatic life* (London: Sinclair-Stevenson, 1994).

Wilk, JR, *The Creation of an Ensemble: The first years of the American Conservatory Theatre* (Carbondale and Edwardsville: Southern Illinois University Press, 1986).

Wheatley, M, *Leadership and The New Science: Discovering the order in a chaotic world* (San Francisco: Berrett Koehler, 1999).

Zeleny, J, 'Obama weighs quick undoing of Bush', *The New York Times,* 9 November 2008.

Zuboff, S and Maxmin, J, *The Support Economy: Why corporations are failing individuals and the next stage of capitalism* (London: Allen Lane, 2003).

Demos - Licence to Publish

The work (as defined below) is provided under the terms of this licence ('licence'). The work is protected by copyright and/or other applicable law. Any use of the work other than as authorized under this licence is prohibited. By exercising any rights to the work provided here, you accept and agree to be bound by the terms of this licence. Demos grants you the rights contained here in consideration of your acceptance of such terms and conditions.

1 Definitions

A **'Collective Work'** means a work, such as a periodical issue, anthology or encyclopedia, in which the Work in its entirety in unmodified form, along with a number of other contributions, constituting separate and independent works in themselves, are assembled into a collective whole. A work that constitutes a Collective Work will not be considered a Derivative Work (as defined below) for the purposes of this Licence.

B **'Derivative Work'** means a work based upon the Work or upon the Work and other pre-existing works, such as a musical arrangement, dramatization, fictionalization, motion picture version, sound recording, art reproduction, abridgment, condensation, or any other form in which the Work may be recast, transformed, or adapted, except that a work that constitutes a Collective Work or a translation from English into another language will not be considered a Derivative Work for the purpose of this Licence.

C **'Licensor'** means the individual or entity that offers the Work under the terms of this Licence.

D **'Original Author'** means the individual or entity who created the Work.

E **'Work'** means the copyrightable work of authorship offered under the terms of this Licence.

F **'You'** means an individual or entity exercising rights under this Licence who has not previously violated the terms of this Licence with respect to the Work,or who has received express permission from Demos to exercise rights under this Licence despite a previous violation.

2 Fair Use Rights

Nothing in this licence is intended to reduce, limit, or restrict any rights arising from fair use, first sale or other limitations on the exclusive rights of the copyright owner under copyright law or other applicable laws.

3 Licence Grant

Subject to the terms and conditions of this Licence, Licensor hereby grants You a worldwide, royalty-free, non-exclusive,perpetual (for the duration of the applicable copyright) licence to exercise the rights in the Work as stated below:

A to reproduce the Work, to incorporate the Work into one or more Collective Works, and to reproduce the Work as incorporated in the Collective Works;

B to distribute copies or phonorecords of, display publicly,perform publicly, and perform publicly by means of a digital audio transmission the Work including as incorporated in Collective Works; The above rights may be exercised in all media and formats whether now known or hereafter devised.The above rights include the right to make such modifications as are technically necessary to exercise the rights in other media and formats. All rights not expressly granted by Licensor are hereby reserved.

4 Restrictions

The licence granted in Section 3 above is expressly made subject to and limited by the following restrictions:

A You may distribute,publicly display, publicly perform, or publicly digitally perform the Work only under the terms of this Licence, and You must include a copy of, or the Uniform Resource Identifier for, this Licence with every copy or phonorecord of the Work You distribute, publicly display,publicly perform, or publicly digitally perform.You may not offer or impose any terms on the Work that alter or restrict the terms of this Licence or the recipients' exercise of the rights granted hereunder.You may not sublicence the Work.You must keep intact all notices that refer to this Licence and to the disclaimer of warranties. You may not distribute, publicly display, publicly perform, or publicly digitally perform the Work with any technological measures that control access or use of the Work in a manner inconsistent with the terms of this Licence Agreement.The above applies to the Work as incorporated in a Collective Work, but this does not require the Collective Work apart from the Work itself to be made subject to the terms of this Licence. If You create a Collective Work, upon notice from any Licencor You must, to the extent practicable, remove from the Collective Work any reference to such Licensor or the Original Author, as requested.

B You may not exercise any of the rights granted to You in Section 3 above in any manner that is primarily intended for or directed toward commercial advantage or private monetary compensation.The exchange of the Work for other copyrighted works by means of digital filesharing or otherwise shall not be considered to be intended for or directed toward commercial advantage or private monetary compensation, provided there is no payment of any monetary compensation in connection with the exchange of copyrighted works.

c If you distribute, publicly display, publicly perform, or publicly digitally perform the Work or any Collective Works,You must keep intact all copyright notices for the Work and give the Original Author credit reasonable to the medium or means You are utilizing by conveying the name (or pseudonym if applicable) of the Original Author if supplied; the title of the Work if supplied. Such credit may be implemented in any reasonable manner; provided, however, that in the case of a Collective Work, at a minimum such credit will appear where any other comparable authorship credit appears and in a manner at least as prominent as such other comparable authorship credit.

5 Representations, Warranties and Disclaimer

A By offering the Work for public release under this Licence, Licensor represents and warrants that, to the best of Licensor's knowledge after reasonable inquiry:

i Licensor has secured all rights in the Work necessary to grant the licence rights hereunder and to permit the lawful exercise of the rights granted hereunder without You having any obligation to pay any royalties, compulsory licence fees, residuals or any other payments;

ii The Work does not infringe the copyright, trademark, publicity rights, common law rights or any other right of any third party or constitute defamation, invasion of privacy or other tortious injury to any third party.

B except as expressly stated in this licence or otherwise agreed in writing or required by applicable law,the work is licenced on an 'as is'basis,without warranties of any kind, either express or implied including,without limitation,any warranties regarding the contents or accuracy of the work.

6 Limitation on Liability

Except to the extent required by applicable law, and except for damages arising from liability to a third party resulting from breach of the warranties in section 5, in no event will licensor be liable to you on any legal theory for any special, incidental,consequential, punitive or exemplary damages arising out of this licence or the use of the work, even if licensor has been advised of the possibility of such damages.

7 Termination

A This Licence and the rights granted hereunder will terminate automatically upon any breach by You of the terms of this Licence. Individuals or entities who have received Collective Works from You under this Licence,however, will not have their licences terminated provided such individuals or entities remain in full compliance with those licences. Sections 1, 2, 5, 6, 7, and 8 will survive any termination of this Licence.

B Subject to the above terms and conditions, the licence granted here is perpetual (for the duration of the applicable copyright in the Work). Notwithstanding the above, Licensor reserves the right to release the Work under different licence terms or to stop distributing the Work at any time; provided, however that any such election will not serve to withdraw this Licence (or any other licence that has been, or is required to be, granted under the terms of this Licence), and this Licence will continue in full force and effect unless terminated as stated above.

8 Miscellaneous

A Each time You distribute or publicly digitally perform the Work or a Collective Work, Demos offers to the recipient a licence to the Work on the same terms and conditions as the licence granted to You under this Licence.

B If any provision of this Licence is invalid or unenforceable under applicable law, it shall not affect the validity or enforceability of the remainder of the terms of this Licence, and without further action by the parties to this agreement, such provision shall be reformed to the minimum extent necessary to make such provision valid and enforceable.

C No term or provision of this Licence shall be deemed waived and no breach consented to unless such waiver or consent shall be in writing and signed by the party to be charged with such waiver or consent.

D This Licence constitutes the entire agreement between the parties with respect to the Work licensed here.There are no understandings, agreements or representations with respect to the Work not specified here. Licensor shall not be bound by any additional provisions that may appear in any communication from You.This Licence may not be modified without the mutual written agreement of Demos and You.